BEYOND THE BLACK BELT

SECRETS OF ADVANCED KARATE RANKS

By

GARY PURDUE

To: Ken Sewell —

Love, Best wishes —

Gary Purdue

ISBN: 0-7596-7240-7

This book is printed on acid free paper.

1stBooks - rev. 3/29/02

DEDICATION

This book was in the early stages of publication on September 11, 2001, when terrorists hijacked four airliners and attacked freedom in the United States of America. The core, the very heart of all we hold precious was assaulted: our lives, liberty and pursuit of happiness were violated.

In light of that dire tragedy, the insights revealed here are even more profound and vital than I originally thought. Those who courageously subdued the terrorists on flight 93 and subsequently died in the crash in Pennsylvania exemplify the ideals portrayed herein, as do the professionals and volunteers who dealt directly with the aftermath of the disaster. They are heroes in the truest meaning of the word.

Beyond The Black Belt is dedicated to those heroes, to those who will follow their example and to all the survivors of the victims on that terrible day. *We will prevail in this time of reckoning.*

ACKNOWLEDGEMENTS

I wrote this book with a *LOT* of help. My karate mentor, James H. Hawkes, the co-founder of the United States Karate Alliance, has been an ongoing example for me. The Trias International Society and Alliance Hall of Fame members provided continued inspiration. If Grandmaster Robert A. Trias hadn't brought karate from Okinawa to the U.S. after World War Two, I would never have been able to take it in the first place.

Colleagues at the University of New Mexico in Albuquerque contributed their support and forbearance. Steve Clapper appointed me to take over the karate club at UNM when he left. Professors Leon Griffin, John Gustafson, Ira Zeff, Todd Seidler and Mary Jo Campbell not only helped me implement karate classes at the University of New Mexico, they supported me through times of cutbacks.

UNM Karate students humbled me with their attention and dedication. They provided many examples I chronicle here. My friend and student Carla Hudson showed me the way to write about the examples.

My family gave me unconditional support during this project. My wife Donna challenged me to finish it. My mother Lois edited and proofread every page. My brother Keith helped ceaselessly to find the best name for this book. My daughter Shauna taunted me when I digressed.

Dave Fishgrab became my second editor at a tumultuous time in his life, just when 1st Books Library appeared like magic to publish this work at the same time I finished writing it. And I thank God, Who allowed me to truly appreciate these friends, relatives and mentors. They led me.

Gary Purdue, 2001

CONTENTS

PART ONE: KARATE RANKS

PART TWO: DYNAMICS and EXECUTION

PART ONE: KARATE RANKS

GARY PURDUE

2

Chapter One

INTRODUCTION

In the beginning

"You got the quarter you owe me?" This wasn't some bum asking for spare change. This was one of the high school football gods demanding tribute from me.

I replied, "Say what?" I didn't owe this guy a dime. I didn't even know him. Everyone at our high school knew him on the football field, but I didn't know him well enough to owe him anything.

He stood glaring down at me with his lieutenant close at hand, two to one against me. He said again, "Hey kid. I asked you a question. You got the quarter you owe me?"

I thought, "Is he kidding? *GOD*, how I hope so." Then I realized, "No! He *isn't* kidding!" Real malice tinged his mocking words.

My seventeen-year-old brain panicked. I was incapable of defending myself in any truly effective or menacing way, and I was terrified. Desperation made me consider ever so briefly, "Do I *have* a quarter I can sacrifice in exchange for my life?"

Before I had a chance to dig through my pockets for a quarter, the coursing panic in me was swamped by an even *bigger* sensation. My fear turned into profound rage as my thoughts exploded, "This punk is threatening me so he can steal my money! *NO WAY!*"

The rage found its way into my eyes. The football thug's lieutenant saw the cold resolve sweep across my face. Turning to his captain, he said, "Hey man, leave the kid alone." The football thug smirked and turned away with a nod. The confrontation ended quicker than it began. I truly had no idea why.

A clear mission in life was presented to me at that moment. Rage or not, I never, *ever* wanted to feel that helpless again.

A few months after that incident my good high school buddy Fred invited me to watch a karate tournament. It was my introduction to karate. Fred was proud that he'd earned his brown belt and wanted me to observe what karate offered.

The discipline and physical grace those empty hand warriors demonstrated at that karate tournament mesmerized me. They exemplified the personal security I desperately longed for. I wanted those results.

So, the rest is history? No, not quite. I contracted a critical case of wanderlust that caused a few other bumpy starts and stops which stretched their tripping feet across my path.

I began taking karate at a self-defense class offered by the Albuquerque, New Mexico Police Department in 1965. We trained every Thursday night. Then after our workouts we watched Bruce Lee kick ass on the television series, "The Green Hornet." Although that class lasted only a few weeks, I gained a skill that served me well for many years. I learned how to ignore fear.

Everyone in the class had to face the other thirty students one at a time. We had to block and counter whatever they threw at us. Plainly stated, the exercise was terrifying! I was suddenly facing *thirty* of those football thugs and they weren't just threatening. They were actually attacking!

Looking back, I don't think anyone in the class thought that facing a line of thirty attackers was a good idea. None of us had mastered anything close to control when throwing techniques. We had no ability to judge distance and couldn't time our blocks or strikes.

Nevertheless, we all swallowed our fear and tried to avoid being seriously injured. The result was incredible.

We all succeeded; there were no injuries. It was a miracle.

Even with that miracle I still wasn't ready to make a commitment to karate. After overcoming that scare I was in denial, and like most young folks, was disenchanted with the city I called home.

4

Albuquerque was a tiny city in the 1960's. Back then as a teenager I was convinced, "There's more to life than what my hometown is offering. Somewhere there *must* exist an exotic, even idyllic place where I can become tough and successful."

I wanted to find the ideal place where I could achieve the elusive "mind-body connection" everyone was talking about back then. Most exotic locations required learning a new language.

I wouldn't delay my case of wanderlust long enough to facilitate that particular feat of language acquisition. I figured, "Australia will be the perfect solution."

After six months of traipsing around the Aussie outback on a hundred-dollar-a-month budget I realized that going "down under" *wasn't* the perfect solution. My dreams weren't coming true at all.

I was homesick. Even worse, I traveled twelve thousand miles and stepped on the *same* kind of stubborn "goat's head thorn" that peppered Albuquerque's landscape.

I gave up my "Crocodile Dundee" dreams before Paul Hogan ever made a movie about Australia. Mom and dad wired the return fare to me and I flew back home.

Have you ever heard the refrain, "Go to school, get a degree, find a career and be a success?" I'd heard that advice my entire life. My dad did it. After my Australian adventure I decided to follow in his path.

I enrolled at the University of New Mexico soon after arriving home. Coincidentally, two friends from the police self-defense class I had attended were teaching at the UNM Karate Club. In January 1967 I began attending their classes four times per week.

What I sought twelve thousand miles away in Australia I found in karate classes right back home. The formerly elusive mind and body connection became tangible and was accompanied by a strong feeling of accomplishment. I was learning new stuff and the new stuff worked!

I was hired to teach karate from a field of four other applicants in 1972, and taught two karate classes daily in addition to the UNM Karate Club at

5

night. Those two initial classes evolved to eleven. I worked out in all of them, a physical commitment of six to eight hours a day.

Karate became the single most important anchor in my life. I finally achieved the physical security that the seventeen-year-old version of me who faced that football thug longed for.

I obtained absolute confidence. Karate does that. If all that wasn't enough I was earning a living by teaching other people how to feel the same glorious way!

Then in 1975 (after eleven years in karate) I received my initial wake-up call, although I didn't recognize it as such at the time. I was sparring an amateur wrestler.

During our match he got behind me, picked me up, then tripped and dumped me on the floor. He landed on top of me.

My shoulder was wrecked and later required surgery.

At that time I was a Nidan, a second-degree black belt. I rationalized, "I got hurt because I treated this wrestler like a novice instead of respecting his amateur athletic skill. That's why I let him get the upper hand."

The shoulder separation wasn't my first karate wound but it was the first time one of my injuries required major surgery. I continued to teach with my arm in a sling, poking fun at myself and performing smooth one-armed forms.

I recovered from my shoulder injury quickly because of my own amateur athletic physical conditioning. But there was another problem; tucked away underneath the reasoning that I used to explain away the injury was a discomforting insight: "My ability and knowledge weren't enough to protect me."

I received my second wake-up call during a tournament in 1978 when I was a Sandan, a third-degree black belt. The day of the match I felt completely in control, omnipotent. My technique, timing and targeting felt unstoppable. "No one can touch me," or so I thought.

During my last match at that tournament I had another thought, "This is too easy. I can score at will on this guy. I think I'll find out how my blocks work on him…"

At the exact moment those arrogant thoughts invaded my mind, my opponent threw a fast spinning hammer fist that hit my right cheekbone. He closed the distance between us so quickly that he caught me completely flat-footed.

His blow shattered my right cheekbone and blew out my right eye socket. My right eyeball was cradled in the blown-out hole of my sinus cavity. It took four hours of expert surgery to reconstruct my face.

It required *decades* for me to come to terms with the emotional results of that moment. I didn't know it then but at the instant my face shattered I began a personal search for answers that no traditional karate school had taught me. They didn't answer my question, "Why did it happen?"

I *HAD* to figure out a way to prevent that kind of injury from ever happening again. That was the real reason I started taking karate in the first place! Simply working out gave me physical condition, technique and targeting, but there had to be more, since all that hadn't kept me from being wasted.

I read and reread every karate book I could find. Occasionally, visualization was mentioned as an effective learning tool for application of karate skills. What did *that* mean?

Only one person was able to elaborate. The first practical advice I learned about visualization came from an ancient tip that my karate friend and mentor Jim Hawkes revealed to me.

His tip came from <u>Karate-Do' Kyo'Han,</u> a book written by Gichin Funakoshi. He took Chinese karate from Okinawa to Japan in 1923. Funakoshi's ancient tip was:

> *True karate, that is, Karate-Do', strives*
> *internally to train the mind to develop a clear*
> *conscience enabling one to face the world*
> *truthfully, while externally developing strength*

until one may overcome even ferocious wild animals. Mind and technique are to become one in true karate.

With that concept I began developing my *own* method for visualization. The process was a slow evolution.

I discovered numerous applications to various techniques in karate patterns by mentally visualizing enemies attacking me in combat. Thus I formed more detailed images of the techniques. The images corresponded to each successfully applied technique in practice. It worked!

That was the missing link. My understanding of visualization expanded and improved as I taught the applications of each move to my students.

I continued to look for examples in karate books but as I reflected on my own experience with my students, I found other questions regarding black belt skills. The classifications of ranks prior to black belt are clearly profiled. (Do *this* form, do *that* move, and you will graduate from white belt to color belt, then to brown belt.) The guidelines for promotion to Shodan (first-degree black belt) are considerably less distinguishable and more subjective.

I had to wonder, "How can I know when to promote my black belt students? I'm supposed to be their Sensei, *not* just a teacher but a leader, guide, and mentor." Translated literally from the Japanese language, "Sensei" means "the one who has been there before." He's an example.

How does a Sensei, the example who has been there before *know* when a Shodan is ready for promotion? How would that "omnipotent one" recognize when a Nidan with the excellence of technique typical of this rank, is ready for promotion to Sandan as a competent semi-professional athlete?

The definable answers I sought were not forthcoming. I mused, "Maybe the answers I seek are long since lost to martial art tradition. Survival itself precludes the open sharing of deadly secrets. Indeed, the answers may be lost to the mysticism enveloping *all* of the Asian fighting and killing war disciplines."

If anyone did know the answers they were *not* sharing them. The "art" aspect of those war disciplines in Asian cultures is a very recent development in history.

Eventually I realized, "Hey! *I'm* a Sensei. I *must* outline a program for black belt rank development. I'm supposed to know how to do that."

But I *didn't* know. If I wasn't able to understand those requirements, my students couldn't prepare for their higher ranks adequately. I didn't want to leave them in the lurch.

Armed with this new objective I began to observe my students and fellow karate-ka more closely. I watched with a deeper and increased awareness.

I discovered that even after allowing for various personality types, circumstances and individual characteristics, a clear profile evolved for each level of black belt rank. The ranks were clearly defined by a list of words not usually associated with the art of karate: need, fear, confidence, trust, ignorance, ownership, balance, desire, frustration, acceptance, expression and most profound of all, confusion.

"Why?" I didn't know why. I was confused as well. I understood those words in a very limited way - but I knew they were critical. I needed to describe those words in stories that would provide examples.

I *had* to provide anecdotes that would show the reality of each black belt rank. That was my vision. My vision gradually became real. In the pages that follow I share my journey of discovery.

The chapters in the first part of this book are dedicated to each level of black belt rank, from first through fourth-degree. These chapters define those ranks physically, mentally and emotionally - and outline a program for advancement to the next higher rank (including fifth-degree and higher!)

The chapters in the second part of this book provide details about dynamics and execution at the different black belt ranks. This section also defines the elements of balance, thrust, speed, impact, focus and harmony as they relate to each black belt rank.

I wish that a book like this had been available when I was a budding young black belt. I could have avoided a *lot* of mistakes!

Carla Hudson helped me write the first draft of this book over a period of six months in 1998. She is a brilliant and *very* talented friend. When she asked me, "What do you want to *do* with this book?"

I had to think deeply. Then I responded, "Expose…" That was all I could say at that time.

"That was then and this is now," as my own daughter told me.

A lot more about karate *and* life than I first imagined is exposed here, and it's for the best. This book is my own personal journey through black belt ranks in karate.

My observations are *not* the most important things you will discover here. I pray that my perspectives will help you make up your own mind about your future. (Not only with karate, but with *all* your resources.)

You may not go through *all* of the examples set down here because of personal maturity, wisdom or enlightenment. You will go through *most* of them, even if you never take one lesson in karate.

I want you to have more of those enlightened flashes of wisdom that guide all of us to our best possible life. You will continue to be guided, as I am, by those people who love and help us. Be very careful to make sure that those who are "helping" you actually *do* have what you want and can really help you attain it.

As I end this introduction I have to make a confession to you, the reader. Every story, every example, every anecdote told here is true. *All* of these situations really happened. I changed most of the names to protect the guilty. I figure the innocents can take care of themselves.

Chapter Two

THE JUSTIFIER

SHODAN (FIRST-DEGREE BLACK BELT)

The Rookie

By noon on Saturday the weekend already felt endless and not in a good way. Ralph paced anxiously around the gymnasium. He paused occasionally to stretch.

His stretching also served another purpose; he could observe the competition. Ralph glanced at his watch. He still had an hour until his first match. Not his first match ever, he reminded himself again, just his first match since being promoted to Shodan.

The first brown belts entered the tournament ring. Ralph eyed the match warily. The first point was scored when one brown belt tagged his opponent with a punch to the throat.

The competitor who was hit seemed fine; he was smiling. Ralph was surprised that the judges allowed the match to continue. "Clearly," he thought, "too much force is being used. Instead of scoring a point the man should have been disqualified."

Ralph had argued with his Sensei about this same issue during the previous night's workout. Remembering that conversation unlocked a floodgate of anger Ralph was trying to hold back since the night before. And to think that the regular Friday night workout had started out so great.

His Sensei had asked him to lead the class. *Finally* Ralph could share his rigorous aerobic exercises that he felt should precede a proper workout. When his warm-up was finished Ralph thought, "The class looks winded, but energized."

Then his Sensei approached and requested, "Would you please continue leading the workout?" Ralph figured he was still on the right track.

He called the class back to attention and announced, "Tonight we're going to work an area too often neglected, basics. In order to improve we all must first master the basics."

Ralph continued. Leading the class felt good. Executing the punching drill in front of the class felt good. Watching students try to mimic him felt even better.

"Yamei." (Stop!) Sensei's command stopped him. His basics were finished.

Before Ralph could ask why, his Sensei explained to the entire class, "Two aspects of Ralph's punch need to be improved."

Ralph was stunned. He thought, "My Sensei just corrected me in front of all these students. He's making me look like a fool!" Ralph blanked out and didn't hear another word uttered. He gaped at his Sensei incredulously.

So many questions ensued from the students that only the half-hour devoted to sparring every Friday night remained when Sensei finished. Since most of the students planned to compete in a tournament the next day the sparring session promised to run much longer than the planned half-hour.

Ralph scanned faces looking for Alice. Not more than three months ago they were promoted to first-degree black belt together.

They agreed completely on what was wrong with their Sensei's teaching methods. They also shared the opinion that Friday night spar parties were becoming very dangerous. Students were allowing their adrenaline to escalate the action until they tagged each other too hard during practice.

Ralph was putting on his gloves when he spotted Alice. She rolled her eyes and shook her head. He knew exactly what she meant and what he feared most didn't take long to occur. In his very first sparring exercise with a brown belt Ralph was popped in the chin. He thought, "That's not much of a blow, but really, the damned fool is out of control."

Worse yet, Sensei was coaching the brown belt and had the gall to congratulate him for penetrating

Ralph's defenses! Then instead of rebuking the brown belt for lack of control, Sensei demonstrated to Ralph how *he* might have blocked the connecting punch! Sensei added insult to potential injury.

For over an hour the students continued to spar, trading out partners occasionally. Ralph caught up with Alice at one point and she confided that she was the only one policing the various matches. Several times during the evening she stopped matches that she thought had escalated too far.

And in every case the students were mad at her for interfering. They all insisted that they were not sparring beyond their abilities. As a black belt she'd known better.

When Sensei called the class to formal bow out he spoke briefly about the upcoming tournament and wished everyone luck. He added, "I also have a special announcement."

Ralph had been completely astonished, "How is this possible? Sensei is promoting Gary to second-degree black belt. Gary a Nidan? Ridiculous, what in heaven's name is Sensei thinking? Gary is no more a Nidan than I'm an…oops!"

There it was again. That nagging thought. Ralph knew, "I should never have been promoted to Shodan. I don't deserve this rank. Sensei really slipped a cog when he came up with *this* one."

Ralph and Alice had discussed this issue to death. Neither of them felt like they were ready for promotion from brown belt to black belt rank. Ralph secretly wondered, "Did Sensei have a gender agenda to fill by promoting Alice? Just maybe I've been added for camouflage."

"But Gary? Promoted to Nidan?" Ralph assumed that Sensei always discussed promotions with *all* the black belts. Judging from the shocked look on Alice's face, Ralph knew she hadn't been consulted either.

Ralph concluded, "If either of us *had* been consulted Gary would *never* have been promoted to Nidan. Sensei really overstepped this time." Ralph planned a few choice words for his mentor.

After the Friday night workout Ralph and Alice went to a local eatery to grab a bite and discuss the situation. Their gripe session lasted late into the night.

As Ralph watched the last brown-belt tournament match at one o'clock on Saturday he was beginning to wish that he'd gone to bed a lot earlier the night before.

Ralph's first and only match of the tournament was over in what seemed like half a heartbeat. His opponent scored two aggressive, lightning fast points before Ralph could move out of his stance. In disgust Ralph thought, "The judges are *idiots*! They didn't control the match at all." Conceding that his opponent might have won anyway, Ralph wished, "After all my preparation the match should have been judged fairly!"

Maybe the day wouldn't be a complete loss. Ralph speculated, "If I can just get Sensei aside for a quiet talk I'll tell him how unsafe sparring has become. I can explain how wrong he was to correct me in front of the class. Maybe I can find out why Alice and I were left out of the loop regarding Gary's promotion."

Ralph continued to ponder, "If Sensei doesn't listen maybe it's time to throw in the towel. After all, I've achieved my black belt. I've perfected my techniques. Not all the applications for my techniques work yet but that's only a matter of time and working out, if it's worth it. Maybe it isn't worth it…" a warm feeling of peace settled his mind once and for all. "Alice had been right. We achieved what we set out to accomplish; we both crossed the finish line."

Ralph's next thought was, "The class has lost sight of our collective goal; it's become too dangerous." By the time he drifted off to sleep the last care left in his mind was, "How will I use all the extra time I'll have now that I don't have to take karate classes anymore?"

Poor Ralph. It's probably a good thing that he dropped out of karate. If he'd stayed with it something most definitely would have happened. He would have learned a *lot* more, but those lessons would have come at too great a cost to his fragile ego.

There are numerous reasons why the art of karate loses so many students at the first level of black belt. Many answers lie in the story I've shared and, one-by-one, I'll uncover the riddles of the rank.

To begin with, Ralph (and Alice too, incidentally) suffered from the "shroud of mysticism" clouding the art of karate. From their first class almost *all* martial art students equate obtaining a black belt with "crossing the finish line." At some point students are told or discover for themselves that there are various and very different degrees of black belt.

From the outside looking in all black belts belong to a prestigious club. Not knowing what those levels of black belt actually mean fosters an endless parade of confusion for Shodans. That's too bad. They have to accept and learn to deal with confusion or quit! Unfortunately, most quit.

Leading the parade of confusion is a Shodan's feelings of inadequacy. Ralph chose an aerobic workout for warm-up because he could excel in front of the class.

And the "basic" drill he chose? Why would someone who already felt inadequate take the risk of executing techniques that he was not secure and comfortable with in front of an entire class? Ah…it's all becoming so much clearer.

Shodans feel that continued repetition of the basics will make them better and to some degree, this is true. But there exists a general feeling among Shodans that they have learned all the techniques they need to know; now they simply have to make those techniques work.

Actually *that* is true as far as it goes. New Shodans have trained muscle memory of basic techniques, but are not yet proficient with application. Because performing the techniques and applying them are two separate animals, new Shodans are uncomfortable during sparring. They are usually easily beaten by other black belts who *are* more comfortable in their roles.

For enthusiastic new Shodans who watch *other* black belts spar and win with vigor, only one conclusion seems to be left. They don't believe they deserve black belt rank. That leaves them with the nagging suspicion that their Sensei doesn't know what he is doing. In extreme cases, Shodans can become quite disrespectful of their Sensei. (Sound like somebody you know?)

When Shodans are not willing to open their minds to new possibilities, they leave or become stagnant. But if they work to overcome their fears and confusion, miracles can happen.

For instance Ron, a Shodan student of mine, decided to find a countermove to my back fist. He worked on making me miss; then he learned to counter with a punch. He practiced the combination of block-and-punch over and over.

At a tournament in Santa Fe Ron competed with a very nasty Nidan and shouldn't have been able to hold his own. Ron used the combination he practiced with me to block the Nidan's kick, then followed up with a counter punch and scored.

Ron developed his first successful trick because he had an open mind. Those who fail as Shodans don't have that advantage. Instead of developing open-minded tricks they get caught up with their own ego problems, doubts and confusion. That's what happened to Ralph and Alice.

Okay, I've explained some of poor Ralph and Alice's concerns. But why would their Sensei allow the class to become so rough and tumble, even dangerous?

Alas, a beginning Shodan does not understand the difference between being "beat," and being "beat *up*." The easiest way to explain those subtleties is to lead you into another story.

You have already figured out that in Ralph and Alice's mind any contact whatsoever constituted unnecessary force. This type of Shodans' over-sensitivity is one end of the scale, and results from their fear of being hurt, their feelings of inadequacy and their lack of application skills. All of this is pretty normal stuff for beginning Shodans, I should note.

Before this chapter is done I'll offer suggestions for moving beyond those roadblocks. But before I do, I'd like to share what the middle of the scale is like. It's a place where complete ignorance of the difference between being beat and being beat up can get you hurt.

Halfway through his tenure as a Shodan, Ron added another trick to his repertoire. He developed a left round kick in addition to his block and punch. He was pretty hot stuff.

At one tournament he had to spar a tough Nidan. After they bowed in, Ron realized that his opponent was standing in range. Ron picked up his left foot and slapped the Nidan in the face with a round kick, thus garnering the first point.

The Nidan wasn't going to take that kind of nonsense from any Shodan. He grabbed Ron's left arm and belted him in the throat with a punch. Ron was choked out for five minutes. The resulting swelling of his larynx ended his (admittedly dubious) singing career.

As a Shodan, Ron didn't recognize how dangerous the Nidan could be. Ron was focused on winning by scoring points and wasn't cognizant of the Nidan's ability to beat him up.

To be quite honest, at that point in his karate career Ron did not yet understand the difference. If he had, he would have realized that his tricks were not enough to hold off the formidable Nidan when provoked. Ron would have played the match in a safer manner. He would have tried to score points while at the same time keeping up a better defense to avoid being slugged in the throat.

This safety issue at first-degree black belt is critical. Without developing safety for themselves during intense workouts they can't compete safely at tournaments. Ron learned that lesson the hard way and it cost him his singing voice. Despite that loss he continued in karate and eventually developed advanced Shodan skills.

How do Shodans become Nidans? They need four major developments.

First, Shodans must learn the importance of physical targets. When they throw a technique and stop it in the air during drills, they don't develop the ability to transfer energy on impact.

Shodans need to work with physical targets, such as striking pads or heavy bags, so they can practice actual contact. Physical targets help students strike with appropriate energy as the situation demands. Shodans will never learn what is too much or too little force without practicing physical contact.

Second, Shodans must learn the function of a stance. The accepted meaning of the word "stance" is contradictory to its true application. A stance is often treated as a pose, but it *isn't* a pose. A stance is the *place between moves*.

Without a doubt our universal misunderstanding of stances comes from karate books full of photographs…those frozen moments in time. (This concept is studied in depth in the dynamics chapter.)

What truly is a stance? If you were to photograph a sprinter running full speed along a beach at the moment one of his feet touched the ground, *THAT* would be a stance. It's the transition between strides.

Like a runner the karateka's stance should be a fluid transition containing balance and using momentum to shift from one movement or step to another. When done right it's pure magic!

Shodans strive to achieve what they feel is the picture perfect stance, only to find out that they can't move freely once they achieve it! Eventually Shodans gain the strength to move with their stances as their leg muscles develop, but they must always keep in mind the true purpose of a stance: it's a *transition* between steps, *not* a pose.

Third, Shodans must face their own feeling of inadequacy. A brown belt is promoted to black belt rank to encourage the growth of their skill and technique. Shodans are not expected to be experts in sparring, kata or anything else for that matter. The first level of black belt is just that, it's the first level. Shodans have learned karate basics and that is a good start.

In order to improve their skills, Shodans need to focus on what they *do* know, instead of thinking about what they *don't* know. When they focus on their weaknesses their own inadequacies will sabotage them. It stands to reason that if you're busy trying to cover up what you don't know, you'll never ask for the help you need. Shodans must learn to ask for help from higher ranks.

Fourth and last, but certainly not least, Shodans have to trust their Sensei to teach them. This trust can eventually develop into an unbreakable bond of loyalty when Shodans learn to accept their Sensei as a mentor. (A Sensei knows more about the ins-and-outs of karate than *all* Shodans put together will ever know!)

As a seventh-degree karateka I *knew* when a student should be promoted. I had my reasons when discussing upcoming promotions with other black belts. Those reasons usually related to finding the other black belts' ability to discern when students were ready for promotion!

Karate is *not* a democracy where every student has an equal vote. Certainly a Shodan can't promote anyone to Nidan rank, or deny a Nidan a promotion that is deserved!

All black belts are not created equal. On average it takes karate students a minimum of three years to travel from white belt novice to their first level of black belt rank. It also takes an average of three years for a first-degree black belt to be promoted to second-degree.

If you multiply that learning curve by third, fourth, and higher level black belt ranks you get an idea of the commitment, skill and aptitude that is necessary to achieve each new level beyond simple black belt.

Let's go back to another challenge, the "beat" versus "beat up" phenomenon. Beginning Shodans are often afraid of being beat, but that is only a matter of losing. Middle level Shodans with a couple of tricks don't recognize, much less understand, that a stronger fighter can (and will) beat them up. How does a competent old-timer Shodan handle the issue? Glad you asked.

Bo was a student of mine at the end of his Shodan career. At his last tournament as a Shodan, he was psyched to spar a dangerous opponent from an out-of-state team that advocated contact and violence. Earlier in the day one of the out-of-state competitors had been disqualified for breaking his opponent's nose.

Bo was faster than his opponent, a fact that worked against him because the judges missed several clean scores when Bo moved lightning quick from one technique to another.

Bo's competitor began to "second-punch," hitting after Bo did. His opponent was much slower but he finally connected on purpose with a cruel kick. The judges awarded the first match point to Bo's opponent.

Bo looked to me for guidance, and I mimed turning up a dial. Bo acknowledged me with a grin. It was time to "turn up the volume."

During the next face-off, Bo connected with a hard punch to his opponent's forehead, snapping the guy's head back and dropping him to the floor. Figuring he would be disqualified for making contact, Bo started to take off his gloves. The judges awarded him a point instead.

The out-of-state competitor was in a scorching rage by the time he pulled himself off the floor. Bo was now at war. He knew his opponent intended to beat him up. There were not going to be any gentlemanly points scored.

Instantly Bo connected with another punch to his opponent's chest. The guy dropped to the floor a second time.

As his opponent struggled to his feet again, Bo knew that the third and final point of the match would have to be scored quickly and cleanly. When the contest resumed Bo's next punch landed on the enraged competitor's solar plexus, knocking him windless as his eyes rolled back into his head and he dropped for a final time to the ground.

Later that same day Bo sparred another member of the out-of-state team. That competitor backed off. Their match was a point competition instead of a blood bath. Bo adjusted his volume accordingly and claimed a clear victory, this time obtained without the "dirt."

Bo then practiced his techniques for months on heavy bags and in one-on-one sparring with his classmates. During that time, he discovered new applications and combinations. Increased leg strength caused his stances to be more fluid. He also learned to seek the guidance of his Sensei in fine tuning his newly acquired skills. All these things together helped him overcome his feelings of inadequacy.

For Bo that was a good thing too, as he was ready to be a second-degree black belt. Bo successfully graduated from Shodan "rookie" to Nidan "amateur" black belt!

Chapter Three

OH, OMNIPOTENT ONE!

NIDAN (SECOND-DEGREE BLACK BELT)

The Amateur

Darkness settles around a small city park in Albuquerque, New Mexico. An occupant meditating in one of the houses lining the streets around the park is jolted to awareness by the blaring arrival of a Chevy, minus its muffler. He watches as seven rowdy young men tumble out of their car doors, cranking the volume on their boom box. The throbbing reverberations crash like waves against rattling windowpanes.

On the way out of his front door, the disturbed Thinker pauses briefly to pick up the only weapon in sight—a mop handle.

The seven would-be thugs barely take note of him before he speaks, "Would you guys mind turning that boom box down?" The testosterone pumps. His question had been issued as a command.

"**&%@ $#&!* (Up yours!)" The leader of the pack is immediately identified by his reply; his curse was not a dismissal. The rest of the thugs quickly move toward the stranger.

The Thinker focuses a cold, penetrating stare at the leader, then addresses him directly; "*You* die first, no matter what else happens."

"Who in hell do you think you are?" Quick to charge to his leader's aid, this thug identifies himself as second in command.

The Thinker fixes his attention on the new voice. "*You* die next. If anybody moves I'll kill both of you."

A ripple of anticipation surges through the group, evidenced by tensing shoulders, shuffling feet, and muffled curses. A third member of the gang voices his

opinion.   "You're a pretty big man with that stick,
^$$-#@((."

Calmly, the Thinker drops his stick aside before he
turns to face all seven thugs again.   The faintest
hint of a smile curls the corners of his mouth.
Indicating with a casual wave of his hand that he's
addressing both the leader and his lieutenant, he
says, "Now I don't have the stick.   I'm still going to
kill both of you if anyone moves."

Seconds tick by, unmarked by comment or movement.
The Thinker leans over, picks up his stick and walks
toward the toughs.   Silently they step aside and let
him pass.

Before the hoodlums jump back into their Chevy and
speed away, the Thinker chortles, "Oh, hell.   You're
just a bunch of chicken-$#)+$."

You have just met a Nidan, a second-degree black
belt.   This rank is a level fraught with danger,
exhilaration and the bully spirit.   In today's world
he would bring a gun to the encounter.   He did that
later in his career.

"But still," you may ask, "why would anyone at *any*
level foolishly confront seven thugs?"   Why indeed:
because unfortunately for Nidans this is the *first*
level in karate where practitioners sometimes feel a
complete lack of confusion - and trust me on this,
confusion can be a *good* thing!

In the previous chapter I outlined the qualities
demonstrated by a student who convinced me that he was
ready to be promoted to Nidan rank.   In this chapter
we will look more closely at the noble characteristics
that exemplify Nidans, and also at their foibles and
follies.

Let's start with what brought another Shodan
student to the Nidan level.   When Ed earned his
second-degree black belt, he was competing in a point
sparring tournament.   During one match, Ed's opponent
threw a spinning back kick.

Ed didn't block, dodge, or retreat from the kick.
I saw him decide that there was a target opening
during his opponent's spin and Ed went for it.

If Ed hadn't possessed amateur athletic strength and skill, he would have been cut in half by that kick. As it was, it took four minutes for him to control his diaphragm spasms before he could continue the fight.

After he recovered, Ed won that fight. Then he won the entire competition. I knew that he was ready for Nidan rank because he exhibited courage, focus, ignored his pain, and had absolute control over his fear.

He did it right and "proved it" to himself. Alas, Ed was also completely ignorant of how dangerous his actions were. Nidans have to continually prove their dominance to themselves.

They specifically develop control to consciously aim and land techniques exactly on desired targets. That makes them feel "right." Unfortunately, when Ed tried to score as his opponent kicked, he missed. Ed paid the price when his opponent moved too fast.

Ed's limited application of techniques worked well as far as it went, but this success is responsible for the main reason some Nidans never progress. It is difficult to give up the security blanket of their "application comfort zone," which may ultimately hinder a Nidan's development, and can also stunt the growth of their students.

A sixth-degree friend of mine mused, "The biggest problem we have in karate is all the Nidans who leave their instructors and start their own karate clubs." Why would that be true? Because for many Nidans, everything else is secondary to their goal of continually proving to themselves how good they are.

When they spar, these second-degrees "thump" their partners to prove they can hit. When opponents score on them, they try to score ten shots of their own to convince themselves that they really deserve their rank.

Ironically, second-degrees' biggest fear is hurting other people. They take karate for protection, yet don't want to hurt others.

What would the solution to *that* dilemma possibly be? Can you say, "Predictability?" When Nidans instruct, they teach techniques and applications that can't be used against them.

You need an example? I can give you one from my own personal files. A few weeks after being promoted to Nidan, I began teaching karate at the University of New Mexico. When sparring with upper level students, I was invincible. The only students who were able to score on me occasionally were yellow belt beginners.

Why? Interesting question. During my many years in karate, I have heard Nidans come up with the most outlandish excuses, reasons and explanations for their failures.

The absolute arrogance of Nidans precludes them from being wrong. Or, Heaven forbid, being at fault.

The most interesting excuse I've been told came from a Nidan who got hit by a Shodan candidate. The Nidan proclaimed, "I allowed that point out of respect for his cultural background that embraces male machismo." (The Shodan candidate came from Panama.)

Yeah, sure, and I thought Shodans were the justifiers! This particular Nidan was doing just fine maintaining his certainty!

Nidans also refuse to lose, to the point where they escalate intensity totally out of proportion to the circumstances at hand. (A Nidan "Thinker" threatening to kill gang-bangers for not turning down their boom box comes to mind…)

But why were the yellow belts scoring on *me* sporadically? They scored on me because, as beginners, they were completely unpredictable! Acknowledging that fact, then seeking answers to it took me to the next level. But there were still many Nidan lessons to learn.

I approached teaching at UNM with the blind arrogance of all good Nidans. I stood in front of each class, showed off with a technique, then repeated it thirty or forty times while the class tried like hell to copy what had passed before their eyes in a blur. Breaking down the elements of each technique to better demonstrate it to students never crossed my mind.

In each class after the basics, I taught combination forms. Then I had the group bow out and went to the next class. I was *teaching*, but I didn't know how to *guide* my students.

As a Nidan, I was only interested in one thing: winning. That's how I could "prove it" to myself. I didn't realize the difference between "demonstration" and "teaching" when I sparred my students. I didn't see that my students wanted me to help them win too. I only saw them as competitors who were trying to beat *me* when we sparred.

That's because commonly Nidans compete with others, instead of competing with the best in themselves. Typically, they see all of their fellow students as competitors who are trying to beat them.

As we discovered earlier, Nidans rest their reputations on their limited ability to apply techniques. They don't yet understand the various dimensions of karate, and because they are victims of their own comfort zones, they don't seek further knowledge.

A Nidan I taught bemoaned the third-degree promotion of a fellow student by telling me over and over, "I certainly have enough trophies, Sensei, to prove that my techniques work."

In the three-hour conversation that ensued, not once did the Nidan ask what he would need to learn for *his* next promotion! He just kept reminding me (in case I hadn't heard the *first* half-dozen times) that his technique was perfect as evidenced by his huge collection of trophies.

Well whoop-de-do. His trophy rewards were a result of his accurate placement of technique. But his idea of perfection was a delusion. Even though Nidans can put techniques where they want them to go, that's *not* all there is to control. Variations in speed, range and impact must also be mastered for correct application. That comes later.

Nidans are also notorious for their tunnel vision. While teaching an evening class of thirty-five students at the University of New Mexico, I decided to focus on repeating techniques. As a Nidan, what I did

was really good. I wanted all my students to learn
what I did, so they could feel really good too!

Twenty minutes into the workout, I looked at the
class for a split second to discover that only twenty
students were left. Ten minutes later I again looked
up and only ten students were left in the class.
Fifteen minutes later, I became aware that only one
purple belt and two brown belts were left.

Evidently, the rest had bailed out due to
exhaustion. From where I was leading the class, the
students had to go around me to leave the workout
room. I didn't see even one student leave! I was
either suffering from tunnel vision in the extreme, or
"Scotty was beaming them up!" ("Captain Kirk - I dinna
think we can take much more!")

Because of the results of such tunnel vision, many
black belts are never promoted beyond the Nidan level.
They never defeat the most formidable opponent they
will ever meet - their own ego. Arrogance prevents
these Nidans from moving forward. So they quit.

I began mentoring Horace, who attained his Shodan
rank in twenty months - two months quicker than I did.
At the time, I was a third-degree and Horace was a
Nidan.

By the time I was a Sandan, I had developed a tough
sidekick. Standing in a very low kibadachi (horse-
straddle stance), I would lift one knee, throw a side
thrust kick, then land without shifting weight or
balance. Of course, speed and practice were the main
ingredients for success. I repeated the exercise for
ten minutes on each leg, then increased to twenty
minutes with each leg. After six months of this
training I developed enough leg strength to do the
kick very, *very* fast.

After watching me work out, one day Horace asked me
how I was able to do my sidekick and I shared the
information with him. Horace practiced for months,
then asked me to spar with him. It was a challenge
and I knew it.

A typical Nidan has three or four techniques that
work all the time. I call them tricks. I knew
Horace's bag of tricks included the right sidekick

that I shared with him. He already had a left back fist and a right reverse punch.

At the match on the following Saturday I scored on Horace at will. I was his teacher and I knew all his tricks. I also knew that as a Nidan, Horace only saw two dimensions in his techniques, the beginning and the end. If someone got too close or too far away, even his tricks were ineffective. He was unable to land anything that Saturday morning and his frustration charged the air between us.

Our match ended when he charged one of my deep stances, then backed off slightly when I discharged one of my trick sidekicks. My kick missed, which was what he hoped for. He charged again, convinced I couldn't throw a second kick from my deep stance.

He was wrong. As soon as my foot touched the ground, I picked up my knee again and threw another kick. I caught him the second time. Gasping for air he choked, "I didn't think you could do that again."

I replied, "Really? Come *on*, Horace! You ought to know I can do *at least* two of those." I showed him my kicking drill…ten to twenty minutes with *each* leg. But when he practiced he *alternated* legs with each kick. Doubling up with that kick was beyond his skill and beyond his understanding.

That moment could have been a turning point for Horace. When he expressed his astonishment at my ability to throw a second side kick from a low stance, I thought, "Maybe confusion has finally returned to his Nidan mind and he's beginning to realize that not everything works as well as a Nidan thinks it does. Maybe he wants some help."

One week later, Horace challenged me again. I guess I'm an optimist. Some small part of me hoped that he was going to use the time to ask for guidance, but when I showed up in my street clothes at the gym on that Saturday morning, Horace was already in his gi (karate uniform) warming up. Noting my attire, Horace asked, "Are we going to spar?

I shook my head in disappointment, "Horace, you don't want to spar me, you want to beat me." He said nothing. There was nothing to say. I was right.

Even he knew it. Horace wasn't looking for a teacher or a mentor. He was looking for tricks he could beat me with.

He was also ignoring his fear of being beaten. Ignoring fear is a device for denying dangers Nidans can cause at this level, as we have seen. It's like the difference in driving to work and not worrying about an accident, versus driving in the Daytona 500 NASCAR Race and not worrying about an accident!

Horace was stuck at Nidan rank trying to prove that what he already knew was all he needed to know. The only growth he had interest in was adding another trick to his bag.

Nidans typically can't find blame in themselves; only excuses. Horace decided that I'd held out on him and hadn't taught him my best techniques. Too bad because I *did* teach him my best techniques. He wasn't able to learn them because of his ego and ignorance.

But at each level of black belt someone rises to meet the challenge. As a Nidan Peter was such a student. He'd been a master of arrogance. He'd submerged himself in a God complex. He'd added tricks to a full bag. He'd driven confusion out of his mind. Then he quit training and dropped out of karate.

Peter wasn't your typical Nidan dropout. He returned to karate training after a ten-year absence. Very rare! He simply worked out, reviewing his skills and fitting in with the program.

Then, quite unexpectedly, he came to me and asked how he could improve. He felt sloppy when sparring lower ranking students and wanted to maintain good form.

I demonstrated how he could change his energy safely at impact by varying the speed of his techniques, "Just slow down and maintain perfect execution. Be deliberate as if you're cutting the crust off bread. It's delightful."

Peter didn't have a clue. For eighteen months he asked questions. He had moments of clarity, obscured by more confusion. Then I taught my ideas about visualization to his class and Peter gained an entirely new viewpoint.

29

That class opened up a whole new "can-o-whoop-ass" for him! First I had the students imagine throwing a perfect kick, any kick. During that mental exercise Peter discovered what had been troubling him about his own front kick and corrected it.

Next I had the students perform a mental kata (pattern) with perfect technique. Then I instructed them to mentally go through their pattern with applications.

Following those mental pattern exercises I had the students spar their *worst* enemy in their own imagination. After these visualization exercises I instructed my students, "Please get up and do any kind of physical workout that you want to do for twenty minutes."

Peter had been focusing for months on developing his ability to fluctuate the energy input of his techniques during sparring. My visualization exercises gave him the opportunity to focus completely on doing that without any physical distraction.

Peter mentally perfected his technique, execution, application and targeting. His learning increased exponentially.

When Peter originally asked me what he needed to do to improve, I asked him how he applied his techniques.

He answered, "When I spar, I challenge my students by staying one level above them. I told you I was doing that, and you said it was okay."

I had to tell him, "Peter, that *is* okay, if you want to spend the rest of your life as a Nidan." I knew that if he continued to spar his students "one level above them" he would *never* be challenged enough to improve his own skills or help his students develop to their next level.

If Peter *really* wanted to master his own "necessary volume control," he needed to apply his skills like a smaller, weaker person. This meant (of course) that he would be scored on. (I can hear *every* Nidan exclaim at this point, "Oh *no*! Heaven *forbid* that somebody can score on *meee*!")

Oh yes. During that process Peter would learn how to *avoid* being hit and scored on instead of simply continuing to score his own strikes.

The fastest way to improve in any activity is by training with people who have better skills. Or when superior athletes aren't available, we can tune down our own skills and energy and practice like a weaker, smaller person. Even when maintaining our best form we *will* lose then.

Nidans *need* to learn that it's OK to lose so they can learn from their losses. When that happens they will lose their excuses. Nidans have a hard time asking for help because they don't feel like they're doing anything wrong.

That was what was so *miraculous* about Peter during my visualization class. He recognized what he needed.

In the purely visual space that Peter had in the privacy of his own mind he transcended two-dimensional thinking. He no longer merely perceived "point-to-point."

He knew *MORE* than the start and finish of his techniques. Peter realized another dimension to his moves. The differences in speed helped him apply techniques at varying distances.

I knew that he was ready for promotion. Peter was open-minded and had the ability to look beyond tricks and techniques.

He stopped looking for a secret recipe. In this new space he was not so sure of himself. Confusion had returned. The confusion was leading him to seek knowledge. He was forming a bond of loyalty with his Sensei in order to find it. Peter was a Sandan, a "semi-professional."

Chapter Four

THE QUESTIONER

SANDAN (THIRD-DEGREE BLACK BELT)

The Semi-Professional

"Why is there always trouble waiting on the sidewalk outside the movie theater?" Rebecca doesn't answer her future husband's question.

He figures that fear has cut off her ability to speak. Parked at the curb is a red Trans Am with a mouthy, vulgar guy at the wheel who's shouting obscenities at the couple. The moviegoer wonders, "What kind of hole has *this* guy crawled out of?"

The catcalls become quite intense as another occupant of the car joins in. All the moviegoer wants is to get Rebecca safely to their car.

His glance in the Trans Am's direction reveals five occupants, not good odds. And suddenly, the moviegoer senses that the danger level has just increased. All five thugs are now catcalling out of the car windows. The moviegoer has to do something in defense.

He takes his turn by calmly saying, "Excuse me. I say chaps, would you kindly cease and desist?" (OK, ok, he actually yelled, "Why don't you guys just shut the hell up!") This response may not cut the tension, but maybe a show of force will clearly state that he will not be a victim. He thinks, "Will this diffuse the situation? Probably not." He's right.

Five big guys pile out of the car. Three mean uglies circle toward his future bride. Rebecca removes one of her wood soled shoes to use as a club. Hey, that's a good idea! But they're looking at the moviegoer.

Two others confront him directly. One is staying back about six feet. It's nighttime and the light is so dim that the only part of him that can be seen clearly is the whites of his eyes. The moviegoer thinks, "If I attack him using the only targets presented, he'll be blinded. Hmmm, that's probably not necessary."

The second thug is six feet, nine inches tall. No exaggeration, he is *HUGE*. The monster asks, "Got something to say, jerk off?" He punctuates his sentence by shoving the moviegoer backwards.

The moviegoer's brain continues processing the information presented. "This monster only pushed me. He didn't punch. We're standing on gravel. The lighting is bad. His legs are too big to kick and he's too tall to hit in the throat. So, his groin is the best available target."

Then offhand, irreverent thoughts come to the moviegoer's mind, "Wait just a minute. I'm with my girlfriend and this monster is with four other guys. Who's the 'jerk-off' here? I'd like to pistol-whip this idiot, but I don't have my gun with me. *That's* a mistake."

As he is pushed backwards by the monster, the moviegoer brings his knee up to test whether or not a target zone is in range. The monster's groin is available but the moviegoer doesn't connect, on purpose.

He's already decided to just turn around and walk away. After all, the monster-man only pushed him. No harm done.

If any real harm *is* intended, the gravel will betray the monster-man if he decides to charge. The moviegoer's knee test revealed that a thrust with his foot would smash the monster right at the target zone. Thankfully, calmer minds prevail.

The monster-man doesn't follow. Both the moviegoer and Rebecca return to their car safely. She puts her shoe back on as they drive away.

You've just met a Sandan; a third level black belt. Compared to the charging-bull mentality of the Nidan in the last chapter, this guy sounds rather calm, wouldn't you say? Right, don't be fooled. (I *know* you aren't fooled!)

The reason the moviegoer was so willing to try the "passive approach" was because of the result of a series of events that were pretty typical of the road that *all* Sandans must travel.

Foremost, Sandans want to be recognized as winners and accepted as experts. Most third-degree black belts are humble about their own accomplishments, but they need to constantly demonstrate how good they are.

In 1976 Roger entered the Central North American Karate Championships, where black belts from all over the continent gathered to compete. Roger had required shoulder surgery seven months earlier.

He used his rehab to prepare for the tournament. Roger was rewarded for his efforts when his mentor promoted him to Sandan only one day before the competition.

Suddenly the CNA tournament became the arena where Roger would prove that he deserved the rank. To add a little more unneeded pressure, Roger had a legend to contend with.

Roger wasn't even *doing* karate when he watched Sandan Jim Hawkes perform for the first time. Roger recognized his future mentor's ability to control violence, safety, fear, and danger.

Roger wanted that control. Now *he* was a Sandan, and Jim Hawkes promoted him. Did Roger really have what it took?

Twenty other competitors vied for the Grand Championship in kata (pattern presentation). Roger won that competition by three points. Could he repeat his success in the kumite (sparring) competition?

Black belt kumite was divided into light, middle and heavyweight divisions. Roger competed in three matches as a middleweight.

In his first match he tried a step-across punch from his traditional practice. Unfortunately the boxing ring they were sparring in was not bolted down. It shifted four inches under the impact of his leg thrust.

It only took Roger a split-second to realize that his customary speed was useless in the unstable ring. Bouncing was his best option but certainly not his strong suit.

Roger was searching for balance with his bounce when he executed a back fist at the exact moment that his opponent picked up his rhythm. His opponent jumped and landed a sidekick to Roger's ribcage.

The force of the kick broke Roger's ribs and knocked the wind out of him. He couldn't breathe.

He learned to deal with this disaster before by completely tightening down his stomach muscles. Roger tightened his torso and exhaled every ounce of air in his lungs.

The spasms stopped. As he continued to tighten his torso, his entire body screamed for oxygen. Thirty seconds passed before Roger could get his breath.

What was he thinking? "Nothing! Nada. Empty mind. Ouch...ugh." (What was going on behind his eyes? Who can say?)

Roger had *no* thoughts, but having his peers recognize him as a Sandan probably helped his determination to overcome the pain of his injury. Roger would *not* go down and he *would* make his opponent pay for that kick!

During the thirty seconds that Roger fought for breath and control, he stayed locked in his stance, staring at his opponent. His opponent's eyes glazed over with fear.

At first Roger didn't know why. Then it came to him, "This guy just landed the hardest kick he's ever hit anybody with and it just bounced off me!"

Roger was still standing and he was pissed. He was sick and tired of cheap shots.

The referee of this match was another legend - Bill "Superfoot" Wallace - but he didn't realize that Roger was trying like hell to pull his breathing into control. Bill instructed, "Well, come on, guys. Fight!"

Roger finally took a long, deep, even breath. He faked a back fist, hoping that his opponent would kindly throw another sidekick. Roger would then have the pleasure of ripping his opponent's leg off.

The desired kick wasn't forthcoming. Roger's long, deep breath completely shattered his opponent's nerves.

His opponent lost both his nerve and his edge. He was telegraphing everything he threw. He went hog wild. In raw panic, Roger's opponent threw a head-level spinning hook kick.

Roger ducked the move with ease and his opponent was left straddling the top rope of the boxing ring. He clung to the bouncing rope, trapped like a fly caught in a web.

Roger thought, "Now you're *mine!*" Just as he started a punch to hit his opponent as hard as possible and knock him completely out of the ring, the referee screamed, "STOP!"

Roger stopped. Bill Wallace had read his mind and wasn't going to give him the two seconds that he needed to knock his opponent's block off.

Roger's thoughts raged, "Damn! I want to *nail* this guy, and he *deserves* it!" He looked at the referee with total frustration.

Roger's opponent untangled himself from the ropes, then stepped up to the line again. Bill Wallace looked at both competitors with his "Howdy Doody" grin.

He was probably thinking, "I've been through all of this before, many times. I'm just enforcing safety."

As frustrating as all that was to Roger, it didn't really matter. He ultimately faked a punch that made his freaked-out opponent flinch, stagger backwards, and bounce off the ropes. That rebound propelled him into Roger's *real* punch, which nailed him solidly on the chin for a knockout. That win was sweet.

Roger won his second and third matches handily. He took the middleweight championship, thanks to Bill Wallace's expert judging. Roger also received the recognition and acceptance that he wanted. Everyone who saw the show knew how badly he'd beaten all of his competition. Grandmaster Robert Trias - the father of American Karate—had a big smile when he remarked to Roger's girlfriend and mother, "Roger did real good, didn't he? He did good all day."

After the tournament Roger had only one regret; he didn't fight the light and heavy weight winners for the grand championship. The tournament promoter didn't allow for that.

Roger still didn't realize the responsibility that would be necessary with his level of skill. He wanted to unleash everything he was capable of doing, and truly had no idea what that was.

As a Sandan, he *did* find out. Not long after this competition, Roger became aware that his girlfriend's stepfather had been abusing her, her brother and her mother.

He knew that a "set-up" was necessary. One evening Roger parked his car on another street so the stepfather wouldn't see it. Then he visited his girlfriend.

Sure enough, her stepfather showed up, drunk. He didn't know Roger was there and was completely taken aback! He was so startled that he actually staggered backwards when he saw Roger.

Roger simply looked at his girlfriend's stepfather. Recognizing his presence without acknowledging that he was human, Roger saw the drunk as nothing but a bunch of targets. (*Lots* of targets.)

The drunk scurried down the hallway to the master bedroom. His wife was waiting there and asked, "What are *you* doing here?" She had official restraining orders to keep him away.

He yelled belligerently, "I'M HERE TO PICK UP MY STUFF!" Roger heard shattering glass and raced down the hall. The abusive jerk had thrown an electric typewriter through the sliding glass doors!

Roger looked at his girlfriend's mother and asked her, "Do you want him out of here?"

"Yes, please," she whispered.

Roger looked deeply into the drunk's eyes, then intoned; "You have two ways to leave. On a stretcher, or run out of here as fast as you can. Your choice, hmm?"

Roger didn't want him to run. Honestly, Roger had a *major* hankering to find out just how lethal he was. Even with his big tournament win he was not quite able to understand his own power.

As aforementioned, Roger did find out - on his girlfriend's drunken stepfather. This sub-human scum abused his wife, stepdaughter, and stepson. He deserved a *major* beating. Roger was handy, able and willing to correctly apply the needed dose of attitude adjustment.

He promptly fulfilled those proceedings when the drunk charged in a frustrated rage. Roger faked him with a low groin punch, then hit his jaw so hard that blood spewed from his nose!

Roger was mystified, thinking "Why is his nose bleeding when I hit him on the chin?" The stepfather was out on his feet, but he shook off the punch and charged again.

Although unhurt, Roger was doused with the stepfather's blood during the ensuing fracas. The drunken jerk scrambled out of the house on his hands and knees, suffering from broken ribs, a black eye and an egg-sized lump on his forehead.

Roger's girlfriend told him later, "When you hit my stepfather I felt the entire house jump and fall a foot! *BLAM!*"

That is *incredible* energy, for simply blasting an idiot who deserves it. It caused an amazing adrenaline rush that Roger needed as a Sandan.

Even so, he restrained his instincts. Roger could have smashed the stepfather with numerous kicks, or rammed his face against a doorframe. Roger chose not to use those moves. He didn't really feel threatened enough to kill his girlfriend's stepfather.

About a month later Roger attended another tournament and realized, "Whatever *it* was that I turned loose to punish my girlfriend's stepfather, I do *not* want to unleash in sparring competition." Whatever that energy was, he knew it should *only* be used against real-life enemies.

It felt very good releasing that same energy when doing kata practice because he could visualize "sub-human predators" who *deserved* that kind of retribution. But Roger couldn't spar anyone for six months because of his fight with his girlfriend's stepfather.

At about the same time Roger was sorting through his puzzles as a Sandan, I was personally confronted with my own previous abuse of strength and skill at Nidan and Sandan levels.

I saw one of my ex-students at the cosmetic counter in a mall retail store. She did really well in my class and I was glad to see her. I asked her, "You were a really good karate student. Why did you stop taking karate with me?"

Her reply was the *worst* testimonial that I've *ever* received. "Gary, your kick broke my ribs when we sparred the last day of class."

Oh my God. I was horrified. I *never* wanted to hurt *any* of my students. Her statement condemned me to a purgatory of unwanted and unexplained injuries, losses and failures that were caused by my own ignorance. I hadn't applied my strength appropriately. I didn't know how, or why.

Third-degrees learn how to "change their volume." They must vary the speed, range, and impact of techniques for safety. I needed to develop those skills in order to help my students spar with me safely.

I sparred my students at the end of each semester for twenty years. When I was a Nidan, I scored points on them at will. As a Sandan, I not only continued doing that but also tried to prevent them from scoring on me. Those were my goals. My students were *supposed* to challenge me so I could achieve those goals.

Mistakenly, I rebuked their challenges hundreds of times. I didn't deal with their challenges intelligently and it caught up with me. When I hurt my enthusiastic students, what was the result? They quit. I didn't want *that*!

I wanted my students to gain my skills and give me their best. Instead of encouraging them, I hurt them and drove some of the *best* ones away *because* they challenged me! When I realized how many students I had lost because of my stupidity, it sobered me. I scared away *hundreds* of my students, and they talked to their friends and relatives.

The students who stayed in my classes because they weren't afraid? Well, they also talked with their friends and relatives. All of them, both those who left and those who chose to stay helped me!

They helped me understand the true meaning of Sandan rank. If I may elaborate, understanding what it means to be a Sandan requires four primary steps.

First, as a third-degree you must release the power you have. Second, you must observe the results caused by your power. Seeing those results is often frightening. Oh, yeah. Be afraid. Be *mighty* afraid. (But not always. Some results are merely disturbing.)

I found this wisdom was a strange concept considering the Sandan flashbacks to my Nidan days. I'm not sure I really helped my students get their best lives by teaching the "same glorious feelings" I had when I was getting it on. I'd hurt too many of them.

That realization led to the third step I needed as a Sandan. I became scared of my own ability. I owned and accepted the ability to scare the hell out of myself. My ex-student with broken ribs revealed that.

Roger exemplified it when he fought and defeated his girlfriend's stepfather. At this incredibly dangerous level we must take absolute, total responsibility for what we are capable of doing.

When he fought against his girlfriend's stepfather, Roger was judge and jury, but he was *not* an executioner. It was only a partial execution. Roger didn't feel threatened enough to complete it. He was scared enough of his own power to stop before he went too far.

Congratulations, Roger! The Sandan moviegoer thanked him for that lesson, because when Roger told him about the blood bath he learned from it. That's why he walked away from the Trans-Am toughs outside the movie house. He knew the fight was pointless.

Roger found out later that his girlfriend's stepfather wanted to attack him with a baseball bat. He told his girlfriend and her mother, "Good. *Let* him attack me with his bat. I *want* him to. He'll wind up looking like a corn dog!"

Roger finally knew his own strength. *That* leads to the fourth step Sandans need. They have to use their strength to develop their *own* brand of excellence! (As Yoda in <u>Star</u> <u>Wars</u> said, "There *is* no *try*. *Do*, or *do not*.") Roger had discovered his excellence and could use it!

I was still looking for mine. The negative testimonial from my ex-student was my third wake-up call. My third call, at third-degree black belt - how appropriate.

I thought about my "intuitive insights" before my first and second wake-up calls. In Chapter One, I mentioned that I was seriously hurt by a wrestler during practice, then smashed by a competitor at a tournament.

While I was in the hospital after the wrestler dumped me, I thought, "I should have listened to that little voice." Surely you've heard those voices too? (I know, I know, if you haven't you're saying, "No, I haven't heard any voices, bub - and don't call me 'Shirley'!")

I remembered a little voice telling me just before I sparred the wrestler, "Get the pads Gary, or you're gonna get *wasted*." With pads I could have smacked the wrestler hard enough to safely stop him from grabbing and dumping me on the gym floor. I didn't get the pads. It was a lesson hard learned. Every time I've ignored that voice I pay for it.

Before my second wake-up call I should have listened to the voices of my friends and relatives. *All* of them warned me not to compete in that tournament! I competed anyway, and got blasted. Facial reconstruction is *not* an item you want in your future. That hurt so much it *really did* scare me.

The third revelation came from my ex-student, and it notified me that I needed to change *BIG* time if I was really sincere about helping others. As a Sandan, I learned to safely vary the speed and distance of my punches, kicks and blocks. With those skills I could improve when training with students of *any* rank.

Slow, medium, fast and full speed power techniques gave me safety when I sparred. I was safe as long as

I could accurately judge my opponents' ability and intentions.

Even as a Sandan I was still hurting people and was being hurt myself because I misjudged others abilities and intentions so often. At tournaments I became frustrated when I scored points the referees didn't acknowledge. How could I make those judges *see* what I was doing?

I *knew* that karate worked. I used it for real, so had some of my students. I thought I was showing that at tournaments, yet my worst injuries came when I was doing karate by the tournament rules. Even worse, my students were getting hurt too. I didn't understand it.

The reason is simple. Sandans think they own more than they actually do. Very few people in *any* arena ever achieve real success, freedom or security in their lives. As a Sandan I felt that I owned those things, when in fact I hadn't earned or experienced them. I had no control over even the simplest things in my life.

For instance, I wondered how many people would take my classes. I had no idea and I never knew. It was very confusing.

Karate tournament sparring rules provide another good example of how Sandans think they own more than they really do. I had both marvelous and disastrous tournament results by the time I was a Sandan.

The reasons for those results became clear to me with more advanced development, but to recognize the reasons I needed more than athletic skill, mental awareness, or emotional adaptation. Most importantly I needed to acquire mental, emotional and spiritual *inspiration*.

I acknowledged that life held and gave larger purposes than I could understand. My supposed control was an illusion. I didn't want to create my own Hell-on-earth involving mistakes and injuries I didn't understand. At times it seemed like I already *had* created it. What I wanted was to develop a safe haven for my most profound desires. I'd never experienced that safety as a Sandan, even though I trained in karate (and for tournaments) for that very purpose.

When I finally acknowledged what karate tournament rules actually are, I was able to put my results into a real light. I could see what was really going on and adjust accordingly.

Karate tournaments have *four* sets of rules for the competitors. (Let's not count spectators' fifth through however many sets of rules! Although they help pay for tournaments, they are only spectators. The *competitors* are the gladiators.)

The tournament promoter lays out the first set of rules for the competitors. Then the referee tries to maintain his second set of rules for scoring and safety. The third and fourth sets of rules are those that each contestant *thinks* will keep them safe during the match.

As a Sandan, I realized that I only had control over my *own* set of rules! The *other* rules were a coin flip. If the promoter didn't care about safety, the judge was incompetent, or my opponent was malignant, it was a *deadly* coin flip that caused me a lot of grief and was miserable for my students as well.

Rules or not, all Sandans tend to think that when they improve, or simply maintain their excellent skills, they won't lose anymore. I trusted that running sprints and long distance (including a marathon) would bring me the strength I needed for security. (Wrong again, Grasshopper! More delusion - Kwai Chang Cain of "Kung Fu" I was not.)

What I wanted as a Sandan was the formula to excel safely. Nidans think they have it, then as Sandans find out that they don't.

When Sandans *accept* that they don't have the formula, they can get on with their development. Then they can enter the Yondan (fourth-degree) level. Yondans understand that it's enough to know how well they do, even when judges don't recognize such excellence.

At the last stage of my Sandan rank, I realized that I would put my life on the line to keep from being injured again, and prevent it from happening to others. I finally acknowledged that I had to treat karate as *real-life*. I couldn't just practice karate as exercise if I wanted to improve further. I also saw that quality in my students when they achieved third-degree.

When I promoted Peter to Sandan, he complained, "I got worse as soon as I was promoted! My techniques are miserable and my forms are sloppy."

In fact, his skill level didn't change at all. Peter simply recognized that he missed more than half the time. He had *always* missed that much, but as a Nidan he couldn't admit it!

When Peter admitted to his inconsistent accuracy, it started him on the path of acknowledging, once again, that karate doesn't work with ordinary rules. I learned that lesson by having my face busted open at a tournament. Peter didn't need to learn that for himself through personal experience. He observed my mistake and wisely learned from it!

When Sandans don't learn from others' mistakes, they have to learn from their own. *That* is painful! At the beginning of Sandan rank, after a comfortable period of seeming perfection as a Nidan, confusion sets in again. This confusion results in new and ongoing questions. As the questions continue, some Sandans long to feel the certainty they had when they were Nidans.

Black belts who are stuck at Sandan level don't want to admit to their confusion anymore and are unwilling to learn from their blunders. Instead, they look for safety zones to avoid the pain. They deny their own fear.

Students stop at third-degree black belt rank because they can't or won't acknowledge the reality of the danger we've seen at this level. They don't want more danger, and they can't progress when they deny their fear of the dangers. These "shrinking" Sandans feel that their rank is too fast and too dangerous. It is. But there IS a way out.

There is only one way to dissipate that "too fast and too dangerous" feeling. To improve, Sandans have to *ignore* their fears, the way Peter did, while he simultaneously recognized the very real dangers and wisely avoided them. This dilemma provided the catalyst for his ability to become used to the confusion and accept it.

By *accepting* the confusion, Peter could then ignore it. With an uncluttered mind he embraced karate physically, mentally, emotionally and spiritually. That lesson *literally* saved his life later on.

As with life, karate is four-dimensional. The only rules are spiritual, but they also apply to the real world. You reap what you sow. At third-degree rank, black belts start to learn what seeds they are planting.

Then with improvement, they learn how to harvest the resulting crop of responsibilities. For one thing, Sandans have to learn how to "be mean" constructively. Peter had to spar two of his Shodan students in order to win his division at a tournament. He asked me, "What do I do here?" At the time, I was a sixth-degree black belt.

I replied, "Beat them." I knew he could do it easily.

Peter looked at me, uncertain. I said, "You're a Sandan. *Show* them that. They need to know how much better your skill is than theirs. *Beat* them."

He did, handily, and instead of being discouraged, they were *inspired!* One of the Shodans commented, "Peter was awesome!" That kind of admiration is the "honey" that drives a Sandan to develop fourth-degree level skills.

For example, Yondans master their range. They can make solid hits to targets at a variety of distances. Average Sandans have to reach out with full extension to hit with power. But Sandans who are budding into fourth-degree skill are learning how to hit with full impact the instant their punch starts. The recognition of such superiority allows advanced Sandans to acknowledge their own potential.

Sandans have mastered the basics. They *are* mastering the applications and they know it! At that time they will be promoted to fourth-degree.

45

When I promoted Peter to fourth-degree, he acknowledged his own skill even further by opening *another* door to excellence. He began helping his students attain the skill he had learned and he showed them how to learn his skill in their own way!

Peter was truly a professional. He was a fourth-degree black belt, a Yondan!

Chapter Five

THE COMMANDO

YONDAN (FOURTH-DEGREE BLACK BELT)

The Professional

Roger competed at the World Karate Championships for his first time in 1979. He enjoyed the company of his Sensei when they visited Walt Disney World in Orlando, Florida after the tournament.

Roger relaxed at Disney World. He relaxed so much that he actually possessed his Yondan rank and reflected; taking time to think about the process he'd gone through to get this far. He'd trained to earn his fourth-degree by running a marathon, a distance of 26.2 miles.

Roger started the race by running his customary 8½ minute per mile pace. He felt very good. The much touted "runners' high" seemed to be working for him.

For the first hour and a half of that marathon Roger felt wonderful, but he thought of the stories he'd heard from other marathon runners, "No matter how good you feel during the race, at the finish line you *will* be wasted."

Roger decided, "If I'm gonna be wiped out at the end of this race anyway, I might as well pick up my pace and see if I can finish faster."

Evidently, the runners' high in Roger's case brought on a vicious attack of stupidity! He sped up and ran 7½ minute per mile paces for the next seven miles.

At mile twenty-one his calf and thigh muscles were cramping. The ripples up his legs caused so much pain he didn't even notice how much his feet hurt. At mile twenty-four, Rogers' right calf muscle tore out. He hobbled to the finish line in agony. He was trashed; he threw up as soon as he crossed the finish line, then collapsed for three hours. Roger finished his one-and-only marathon in three hours and fifty-seven minutes.

Roger didn't die, as the warrior who ran the first marathon in Greece did. Roger did lose five toenails because of poorly fitting running shoes. That marathon taught him two important lessons that spilled over into his understanding of karate and life.

Roger realized, "I can maintain the correct pace I've learned. That way I'll finish faster. Or I can speed up and get wasted. I messed up. I chose the wrong pace." {He also chose the wrong shoes.} Roger realized that he should have stayed with the pace he knew; with his 8½ minute per mile pace he'd have finished the marathon faster while avoiding the injury and exhaustion he suffered by speeding up.

The most important lesson Roger learned during that marathon was one I mentioned in Chapter One. That lesson changed the way he perceived the role that karate played in his life.

Roger realized that he should take advice *only* from people who already have accomplished what he wanted. He needed to ignore the losers who liked to moan. Indeed, *all* of us need to learn from good counsel.

Roger took the lessons he learned during that marathon to his first World Karate Championships. When practicing the day before competition started, he discovered new applications for all of his moves and combinations. He was pumped!

Roger later showed me an example as he demonstrated a basic technique saying, "I realized that this simple rising block with my forearm could do more than simply block some guy's punch."

Roger then demonstrated how to trap an attacker's wrist with one hand, jam a rising forearm into his armpit, then lever his arm into a submission hold! Roger added, "Those new applications came in a flash. I guess life is like that. Nothing new comes for days, maybe years. But when I practice with patience and accept God's guidance gratefully, I know I'll eventually receive a *flood* of new insight."

Roger's new insights distracted him when he competed in his first World Championship tournament.

Exciting as all his new applications were, he didn't know them well enough to demonstrate confidence or consistency. Even so, he placed fifth out of the sixty black belts there.

That was a good start for Roger's international competition. He acknowledged his lifelong commitment to karate excellence as a professional. His improved understanding was more important than winning one tournament.

We all see international sports on television as spectators. We enjoy the beauty of victory. We watch superior athletes win at Olympic Games and applaud. We see Tiger Wood's domination in his arena of professional golf and admire his supreme dominance.

For most people, admiration is as far as they can go. Fourth-degree black belts go far beyond the mere observation of admiring spectators. Yondans attain their highest achievement as professionals in their personally chosen fields of expertise, even when *they* don't win.

When I was a Yondan I coached my own daughter in karate. She competed as a junior beginner at the New Mexico Invitational Championships held in Santa Fe in 1981. Her first match was fast and out-of-control. Shauna scored the only match point when she kicked her hapless opponent's groin while simultaneously punching him in the face. She knocked him ten feet out of the ring. Not bad...

I observed her next opponent very carefully; he was hammering his opponents on their heads. He hammered very *hard* on their heads because he outweighed them by more than forty pounds.

I was worried about Shauna's safety in her match with "The Hammer," and prayed, "Please keep her safe." I noticed the referee whisper something to him before the match began.

The Hammer was gentle with Shauna. He used the same techniques that he clobbered his opponents with previously, but he deliberately missed Shauna by inches.

Of course, Shauna lost the match - but she was *thrilled* that she wasn't hurt. She bounced up to me

49

holding her trophy and announced, "Papa, I won second place - and he didn't even *hit* me!" We were totally relieved.

Later during the tournament I asked the referee, "Please tell me what you whispered to my daughter's opponent before their match?"

He grinned at me conspiratorially and replied, "I told him, 'This is Gary Purdue's kid. You know him. He does those scary knife forms. If you hurt her, he'll *kill* you.'"

I was pleased. His threat kept my daughter safe! That was as it should be. As a Yondan my name was being used to threaten and teach other people to do the right thing.

That was a just and fair use of my name. Another example of "righteous intimidation" is appropriate here.

When fourth degrees teach, they have a command presence that is unmistakable. During one of his classes Yondan Peter asked, "Why are all of you throwing your kicks like robots? Just last week you learned how to kick smoothly. You *know* how to kick correctly, what's up tonight?"

None of his students answered him. One student *did* have enough courage to look at Peter directly.

Peter questioned this student about the problem, and received a sputtering response. (As Porky Pig of cartoon notoriety would say; "Bdeea-bdeea, that's all folks…")

While observing this scenario I realized that all of Peter's students feared incurring his wrath by giving a wrong answer! ("Oh no, we don't want to tick off Sensei!")

Actually there was no danger of that. Peter only wanted feedback to help his class improve. His students misread him. They were used to other teachers who became irritated because students didn't learn quickly enough. (I had done that with my "Beam them up, Scotty" teaching style as a Nidan.}

When third-degrees are teaching and want to make a point, they intimidate on purpose. Peter did that to his Shodan students at a tournament when he beat them so easily.

Peter was now a fourth-degree black belt. When Yondans teach, they intimidate unconsciously (irritating though it may be.) Because of fourth-degrees' raw professional power, students automatically pay attention. Yondans can help their students surpass self-imposed limitations and achieve their highest dreams.

Peter broke the usual Shodan mold when he mentored an unusually enthusiastic female student. He helped Mariana develop so quickly that she beat the reigning fourth-degree world champion twice, as a *brown* belt! Mariana then beat that champion five out of seven times after being promoted to Shodan.

Peter helped Mariana accomplish her victories in less than three years by teaching her the drills I assigned to him for his improvement as a fourth-degree. Some of the positional work I assigned to Peter for his Yondan development was very advanced, but he was able to break it down into simple steps that Mariana learned quickly, if not easily.

One of the drills required double and triple shifting, then explosive target acquisition. Peter taught Mariana how to do the drills at the same time he was learning them. I was amazed!

I joyfully watched Mariana compete and win as a rookie black belt, because Peter made sure she "got it right." She did get it right. Mariana won the Women's Black Belt sparring grand championship at the 2000 U.S. Karate Alliance Nationals. She defended her title with improved style and grace in 2001.

The "get it right" mentality helps fourth-degrees develop a highly refined sense of justice. This attitude can lead Yondans into law enforcement, and may cause them to look for trouble. Of course, they usually find it.

Yondan Roy might have asked, "Why is there always trouble brewing *inside* the movie theater?" He was sitting with his girlfriend and daughter on either side. Most of his karate students were seated in the same row.

A seedy-looking individual in the seat directly in front of Roy had just finished a beer, tossed the can away, and lit up a cigarette. Roy decided on polite intervention. After all, he'd been a police officer-in-training for six months.

He wanted to test his command skills. "Excuse me sir," Roy whispered, "You're not allowed to smoke in this theater. Please put out your cigarette."

"El Seedy" spat back, "Screw you, pal! I'm smokin' and you can't stop me!"

Roy immediately slapped the back of the smoker's head, telling him, "Put out that smoke *now!*"

The smoker leaped up with a growl and swung around spraying cigarette ashes. His fist clipped off Roy's glasses. As Roy stood, he felt his adrenaline gland open with a "snap." He drilled his right fist onto the smoker's chin. When El Seedy didn't collapse from that first punch, Roy felt a *second* adrenaline rush snap into his head. Pop… *POP!*

The smoker threw wild haymaker punches. Roy avoided the windmilling fists by bobbing and weaving, boxer style.

For every third or fourth punch that flailed by, Roy nailed El Seedy on the nose and mouth with an accurate jab or hook. "What the Hell is going on here," Roy thought, "why isn't this idiot dropping?"

As he continued to dodge blows and punch the smoker, Roy surmised, "This slanted theater floor and row of seats between us prevent my punches from having enough power to subdue this jerk." (The truth is revealed later in the chapter about thrust.)

The theater was crowded with other team members who were craning their heads to check out the action. The squad directly behind Roy wearied of the interruption. They wanted to see the jail escape scene as <u>Rambo: First Blood</u> continued to play on screen, and pulled Roy into his seat.

The smoker didn't stop his antagonism; he continued to curse and throw punches, so Roy stomp kicked him in the face while being held back. Roy's girlfriend tried to intervene, saying, "Hey, calm down. Don't attack my friend. He's a fourth-degree black belt."

Roy's daughter told him later, "Oh *brother*! That was a real *bonehead* thing to say!" She was right of course; the girlfriend's comment enraged the smoker even more.

When he noticed Roy's police telescope baton he became even more agitated. The smoker screeched, "You've got a club! I'm calling the cops!" He leaped up to call the police. Roy removed the baton, handed it to his daughter, and calmly waited for the law to arrive.

Roy could tell that the smoker really talked up a storm. When the cops arrived, they were *very* wary as they approached. Roy asked the officers, "Are you looking at me?" (He thought of Robert DeNiro's line in the movie <u>Taxi</u> <u>Driver</u>.)

The police officers acknowledged his reference and escorted him to the lobby. Roy decided not to tell them he was a cop, and responded like an ordinary citizen.

He wanted to use the incident as an example to teach his students. They needed to learn correct response when being questioned by police officers.

Roy walked up to the smoker, stuck out his hand and said, "Hello. My name is Roy and I'm sorry for all this trouble."

The smoker distinguished himself as the troublemaker when he cursed and said, "I ain't shaking your damned hand! You hit me!"

One of the officers immediately cut the smoker off by commanding; "*YOU SHUT UP*! You've given us your side of the story. Be quiet and let him tell his side!" The smoker fell silent.

Roy completed his version of the incident; "The smoker started swinging at me, and I protected myself."

The smoker interrupted, yelling out, "He had a weapon! Where's his weapon?"

Roy looked at the officer and said, "He must have seen my belt buckle. See? It *looks* like a Colt .45 pistol."

The cop looked at the gun-shaped buckle and nodded. One professional to another, he said grimly, "Yes sir, of course."

The officer then directed his attention to the smoker, informing him, "You can press charges for this assault, but it'll cost you fifty bucks." He told Roy, "You have the same option, sir."

Roy gave the officer a knowing glance and said, "I don't want to bother doing that. Besides, I don't even know this idiot's name."

The officer replied, "I can't tell you that," at the same time he peeled back his police report to the page with the smoker's name revealed! The cop winked at Roy.

Roy winked back, acknowledging, "El Seedy. Thank you officer." Roy would remember that name and face.

The officer nodded, pursing his lips to maintain an officially grim countenance. He didn't want to smile.

"Hey! I don't know *his* name!" The smoker interrupted.

The officer looked at El Seedy with disgust, then rasped, "This man told you his name when he *tried* to shake hands with you earlier. You don't remember it? Too bad."

Roy shook hands with both officers, and thanked them. They sounded like "Robocop" when they responded, "Thank you for your cooperation. Stay out of trouble."

Of course he wouldn't! After the officers left, Roy went to the men's restroom in the theater. The double dose of adrenaline had done a number on his stomach. He entered one of the stalls, closed the door, and threw up. While he was occupied so unpleasantly, Roy heard the smoker come in and wash off his bloodied face.

Roy had the urge to sneak out of his stall and smash El Seedy's face into the sink and faucet. "Nah," Roy thought. "This incident must end here and now. Besides, sneaking isn't my style."

A week later, Roy decided to check out the movie again with his mother, daughter and girlfriend. After all, he missed half of the movie while dealing with El Seedy and the cops.

As luck would have it, just before the movie started some guy in a wheelchair lit up a cigarette right in front of Roy, who leaned forward to object. His mom leaped up to find an usher. She didn't want the previous incident repeated.

Roy whispered, "Hey guy. You can't smoke in here, OK?"

The wheelchair smoker turned. Startled, he said, "Sensei? I'm sorry. I would never bother *you*!"

Roy's mom returned with an usher. She was amazed to find that the smoker was one of her son's students, and relieved that the situation was already resolved peacefully. That's Yondan for you; fourth-degrees teach a lot of people.

Yondan Roy had been a police officer for a year teaching good guys (and arresting bad guys) when he reminded me of some advice I'd offered when he graduated from the police academy; "Roy, your rookie enthusiasm is natural. I also know you will eventually tire of all the crap that criminals dish out. When that happens, I want you to tell me about it."

Roy told me, "Sensei, you said it would happen, and it did. I snapped on a crook today. I arrested this guy, and he was yelling at me, threatening, 'I'm gonna kill you! I'll slaughter your wife, your friends and your dog.'"

"So I pulled my squad car over, took off my badge and removed my gun, then told the dirt-bag to get out and take his best shot at me. Of course, he was all mouth. He didn't want any real action and begged me not to hurt him."

Roy didn't hurt him; instead, he pinned his badge back on, re-holstered his weapon, and with a great deal of disdain drove the silenced dirt-bag to jail.

Roy finished recalling the incident and revealed, "I felt like Jack Lord playing Steve McGarrett in the longest running police drama on television, "Hawaii-Five-O," when I said, 'Book him, Danno.'" Indeed.

I was amused, as I congratulated Roy on both his personal response and his professional restraint. I commented, "You are definitely over your phase as a rookie." As a Yondan *and* as a cop, Roy epitomized a true professional, but he was still human.

That positive human side will prevent some Yondans' promotion to higher ranks. The feeling at fourth-degree is "OK, I'm confused. So what? What I do not only works great, but I'm improving as well. I'm used to doing this, and I enjoy it *a lot*."

Fourth-degrees no longer ignore or deny the results of their actions. They accept those results. They *embrace* those results, to the point that advanced Yondans are *comfortable* with their confusion!

Beyond fourth-degree, higher ranks are distinguished largely by their overall contribution to karate. It's simple to work out and improve. Teaching this to others is more difficult, but is also more rewarding.

Advanced Yondans develop programs that show their black belts how to improve. When Yondan Peter asked me what I thought about one of his student's promotion to fourth-degree rank, I replied, "That's up to you, whenever you think he's ready. I have no problem with it right now."

Peter asked, "Why do you think he's ready?" We re-read the final pages of my Sandan manuscript.

Peter observed, "I still have a problem. He wants to spar the way I do with students. To do that, he needs to spar at slow or medium speed, allowing safe and solid hits. But he still fast-shoots his techniques and gets 'the-hell-outta-Dodge' to insure his safety."

Peter and I checked out the Sandan manuscript chapter together, and found the missing link for what his third-degree student needed for promotion.

Upon review, he needed to learn how to vary his speed, range and impact. By developing those skills, Peter's student could hit and be hit safely. What a formula for success!

Peter's student already proved his ability to shoot techniques at full-speed. By decelerating on contact

56

he could stop his punches and kicks with a safe "feather touch" whenever his opponents presented viable targets.

He needed to use slower speeds to help other students develop safely. Peter and I discovered specific keys to help him achieve the skills necessary for his fourth-degree promotion!

Let's see; Yondans have personal, continual and successful development, coupled with the deep enjoyment they earn by mentoring other students. Doing all that can be so satisfying that Yondans don't care about further promotions.

This is heady stuff, and fourth-degree isn't a bad place to stay. Yondans can become so immersed in the dual satisfaction of self-improvement and helping others that "upping rank" becomes meaningless.

Peter wanted more than that, and got it. He shouldn't even have been at the UNM Karate Club when he helped me answer the questions I had about Yondan advancement. He spent the day at a medical examination; it was embarrassing, inconvenient and painful.

After the customary bow-in ceremony I advised Peter's students, "Appreciate what Sensei Peter is going to teach you, in light of the fact that he is here despite a personal ordeal."

His students acknowledged my comments. Peter proceeded to teach how to kick with advanced combinations. He then taught how to successfully kick elusive opponents.

He *almost* hurt himself demonstrating… (*Do not* fully stretch with kicks when you've just had several feet of tubes exploring inside you. Unless you're a Yondan, your guts can't take it. Peter's guts *did* take it. He was *that* professional!)

In that one class, Peter helped reveal what his Sandan student needed for promotion to fourth-degree, then taught successful kicking combinations to the class. In addition, at the exact time I was writing about Yondan transition, Peter had a question that helped me recognize how I could teach the transitional skills that he needed for *his* next promotion!

He asked, "Sensei, *every* student I spar at some point accelerates and smacks me in the mouth. I'm *tired* of it. What can I do to stop them from hitting me?"

We both knew that if he increased his speed he would dominate and discourage his students. That was unacceptable. Sensei Peter's students knew that he could hammer them at will, safely, and they tried to do the same against him. That was what sparring was all about.

Peter also knew that his dominance *pulled* those full-speed moves out of his students. They hit with no injury, but it still bothered him because they were out of control.

As a seventh-degree I knew the answer to help him. I instructed, "Peter, you have to work your head and torso movement at fast-to-full speed. Bob and weave your head at least three-fourths full speed, even when you are throwing your techniques at slow-to-medium speeds for safety. Does that make sense?"

Peter paused. He looked away in his mind's eye and visualized the solution I presented. "Yes," he said, "but I have to do two other things before I can accomplish that. First, I have to accept that my students *will* at some point shoot full speed at me, because I draw that out of them. I have to *always remember* they are going to do that. Second, I have to be ready for those full-speed shots. I must *anticipate* those shots!"

"Then, I have to develop what you said. I have to move my head and body *faster* than I kick and punch when I spar my students. That's a really tough assignment for my concentration, focus and intensity."

He smiled. "I didn't realize I would get this tough an assignment as a fourth-degree! Well, whatever. I need to progress."

Peter not only recognized what he needed to improve as a Yondan, but he simplified the challenge into simple steps! Personally, I hadn't been able to do that even as a seventh- degree because I took the preliminary steps for granted. We were working together with perfectly timed purpose and vision!

Peter was the *first* Yondan I ever taught who asked me how they could stop students from hitting them, "Because it was getting really old." *None* of the other Yondans I taught thought deeply enough to know that it was a problem. (Or they were still ignoring that problem!)

I solved that problem for Peter when I demonstrated the body and head shifting he needed. When he simplified that solution, he helped answer another question I was asking: "Why doesn't Peter have 'the look' of total resolve? I *know* he's capable of having that gaze…" and I thought of an example I had seen of the look I expected from him.

As a police officer working at the New Mexico State Fairgrounds, Roy thought that he had seen it all. He hadn't, and he was too far away to stop the assault at the rodeo. He witnessed a burly six-footer *demolish* a skinny five foot tall cowboy with a really good combination.

The big cowboy smashed right and left punches to the smaller cowboy's chin, then kicked his chest. When that kick landed, it sounded like a watermelon smashing against the ground.

Good combination, but given Roy's presence it was definitely the wrong timing. Roy knew of *no* excuse for that kind of abuse. He moved in.

Two cowboys had already moved in and grabbed the "Big One's" arms. He was still yelling and screaming at the poor demolished soul.

Roy snap punched the big cowboy on his chin, to hopefully quiet him down. It didn't work.

Even worse, the whole crowd watching saw a cop hit a "restrained guy" in the face! "OOOOOAAAAAHHH!" was the crowd's reaction. Roy knew that he'd just made a *huge* strategic blunder.

He had also been recently promoted to fifth-degree black belt and knew how to compensate for his mistake. Roy told the two cowboys holding the Big One, "Let him go!"

"What?" The two cowboys were dumbfounded. "What?" Roy looked into each cowboy's eyes as they held onto the Big One's arms. He saw incredible fear in their faces.   He also detected the rage in the Big One's eyes.

Roy relished this challenge.   With an incredible calmness he commanded a second time, "Let him go!" The two cowboys sprang away, releasing the big cowboy. He hauled back and started to smash his fist onto Roy the same way he'd smashed the poor cowboy before - and probably smashed everyone else in his life.

Roy looked directly into the big cowboy's eyes, then gave a *final* command to him, "Don't do it, buddy!"

The Big One melted like butter.   His rage evaporated, like a balloon leaking air.   He'd looked into the eyes of death, and wanted no part of it.

Roy then performed his *own* good combination - one he'd learned from Roger.   Roy snapped his hand onto the cowboy's wrist, then jammed his forearm into the Big One's armpit and cranked him around.   Roy had total control.   He escorted the big cowboy out of the rodeo.

It's good to have quality backup, and Roy enjoyed his Sensei's assistance when they tossed the bum out. As the deadly duo turned to face the awed onlookers, they felt like tipping their hats and singing, "Hit the road, Jack, and don't you come back no more…"

I knew Peter possessed that skill.   I saw him teaching it to his students.   Why didn't he have the "look" that Roy manifested during his incident with the big cowboy?   Why didn't Peter *know* he had that capacity?

And then it came to me!   When Peter accepted his assignment to train his body-and-head-shifting *safely* against his students, they would *never* be able to smack him the mouth again, *never*.

That was what demoralized the big cowboy against Roy.   Roy showed no targets.   All the cowboy sensed was Roy's *total* deadly killing commitment aimed directly at him!   The cowboy couldn't handle it.   He folded like a gambler with a lousy hand of cards. That's what pros like Roy and Peter can do to lesser opponents.

Armed with his newly improved positioning, Peter was not only elusive on defense, he was *overpowering* on offense. It's as if he was juggling with all of the balls in the air. Advanced fourth-degrees' opponents have to deal with too much of everything to keep up with such skill!

Peter tested his assignment while sparring with a good friend who was also a fourth-degree. Peter shifted, then trapped and countered one of his buddy's punches in a novel way.

His friend exclaimed, "Where did *that* come from?" Peter just smiled. He knew he could do those moves at will.

Peter was also teaching selected black belt students how to move with control in fights. He trained himself and his chosen partners at safe speeds - from slow to medium, then up to fast speed - while working realistic sparring.

While Peter trained his shifting skills he automatically gathered intensity and focus. He felt like the "Ghost" and the "Darkness," those two man-eating lions in East Africa's Tsavo Valley.

If you've never seen that look, check out Michael Douglas' excellent movie about the incident. Those lions killed more than one hundred and thirty men back in 1898... yeah, really. I quote from Samuel at the end of that movie, "If you want to see the lions today, you must go to America. They are in The Field Museum in Chicago, Illinois. Even now, if you dare lock eyes with them, you will be afraid."

The committed focus and control Peter learned as he developed that kind of certainty would give him the Ghost and the Darkness gaze. When he stopped shifting, Peter would "laser-beam" his focused intensity into the eyes of his opponents. He would own the look of total, deadly dominance.

In reality, Peter would feel undefeatable. His opponents would be his prey. As his prey, they could only recognize and accept their fate in the same way that crippled gazelles accept death at the teeth and claws of lions, leopards and tigers.

That look is unforgettable. It is harsh, penetrating and absolute. It is the *utter* conviction that you see in their eyes. You will see their real vision of unstoppable rampage and destruction.

Or, if you are lucky, you will see their real vision of complete beauty and creation. Either way, I knew when I saw *that* look in Peter's eyes - *he* would be my first official fifth-degree black belt. He would be a Godan, a *super*-pro!

PART TWO: DYNAMICS and EXECUTION

GARY PURDUE

Chapter Six

DYNAMICS

ESSENCE

We're ALL Black belts here. Let's get this right.

While writing this book I came to realize that even as a 7th degree black belt, I didn't know it all. Carla was helping me write the first draft of this book and commented, "Hey Kyoshi, you're supposed to be a master teacher of teachers. You're a wizard, right? Yet even with all your decades of personal expertise you still need help to get the best in your own life."

She busted me. All I could say was; "You're right. I'm learning from others who have more experience. Most importantly, I'm learning from others who attained more success."

She nodded, then asked, "So?"

I acknowledged, "I want to pass that information on by writing this book. I can clarify and simplify karate. Others will wisely achieve their best success by building on my experience."

Maybe I could discover what I didn't know about karate by looking closer at black belt ranks. Some of my best students had the courage to ask irreverent questions. One of them asked, "How can I learn this karate stuff as fast as possible?"

He was only a beginner, but he had a good question. I replied, "Learning karate *fast* isn't the solution. Even working out *hard* isn't enough. If you will permit me, I have a couple of questions for *you*. Why do we *do* karate the way we do? How can we use karate properly?"

My questions hammered him and he quit. Thousands like him quit. They couldn't come up with any answers.

I probably offended them or they needed something I couldn't provide. Maybe they were scared or lost interest. I didn't know. Whatever the case, they weren't the right fit for karate.

I remembered what Confucius said; "The wizard to one is the humble servant to another." I wasn't trying to be cruel or mean. I was trying to enjoy my life, help people achieve their best life, and be funny with my second list of karate questions. The words I came up with to answer my own questions was another traditional karate list.

My second list included: stance, set, snap, power, speed, range, thrust, impact, intensity, balance, concentration, focus, vision, justice and harmony.

I related those words to the way we execute karate moves properly. In karate we had a problem.

Karate history created several unusual obstacles. Original karate masters are unavailable via modern communication systems. (After all, they're dead. Of course, you *know* that.)

Regardless, even when they *were* alive, the ancient masters were secretive. They *had* to be secretive for their survival.

Hundreds of years ago they passed their skills on to a small number of trusted students. Some of those students wrote books with drawings that showed the wisdom of their ancient masters. Through language barriers those cryptic pictured interpretations defined karate method. We've learned it that way ever since. Our karate origins continue unchanged, despite any personal instruction or insight.

All these centuries later we can trace our karate origins. We inevitably find they are based on marvelous (yet miserable) black and white photographs and stick figures displayed so prominently in the books written by the ancient Masters and their students.

Those images are marvelous because they endured through the ages and reached all of us in karate today! So why do I also call those images *miserable*?

Because we not only didn't try to interpret the pictures in new ways, we didn't even try to understand them in the *first* place! All we did was try to copy the pictures with our own bodies, like children mimicking adults.

Can you think of a coach in *any* other athletic endeavor trying to teach agility, balance, movement and power from ancient frozen images in books? Imagine past gymnastic coach Bella Corolli using a book to teach Olympic Champion Nadia Comanechi how to perform the first *perfect ten* gymnastic score in Olympic history from pictures. (She actually received a score of 0.00. In previous Olympics, gymnastic judges scored competitors up to 9.95. They had never acknowledged a perfect 10.00.)

Let's use an example from today's athletics. Think of Earl Woods using pictures to teach his three-year old son Tiger how to strike a golf ball. It would never happen.

But we attempted that in karate. We tried it all the time. One of my Shodans exclaimed to me, "Look, Kyoshi, I'm in the same stance that the fourth-degree in this picture has! I can't *move* but I look like the picture in this book! *Now* what do I do?"

The pictures my Shodan student mimicked were our first karate teachers here in the United States. We've used them to our dismay ever since. Even the newest videos and DVDs about karate are based on those old photos showing static positions.

I reviewed a video copied from 1924 movie footage showing Master Gichin Funakoshi working out. His comments about "developing strength until one may overcome even ferocious wild animals" provided me with my most fundamental understanding of karate application.

The video showed him moving from one pose to another, just as I'd learned and taught. Disconcerting.

With all our modern technology we were still firmly entrenched in the traditional karate dogma, "Look at this pose. Feel it. Do it." It became even *more* disconcerting.

After a three-decade process of doing traditional postures, I realized that the terms karate *had* given us only supported our ignorance. Words like *stance* and *set* took on the static feeling of being rooted to the floor.

Those words cemented our misunderstanding of the frozen images we were trying to copy. We were trying to look like statues!

Ironically, the very definitions of the words we were using precluded us from obtaining the answers we needed. We were misled, bamboozled and hoodwinked.

We never asked any questions because we thought we already had the answers. Our karate dogma was a traditional ritual of limitation.

I didn't ask about karate dynamics or applications because I accepted the dogma without question. I learned techniques by faith and simply imitated the poses my first Sensei showed me when he said, "Do this."

I wondered, "*Why* do this? Why does karate really work?" I never actively asked. I learned to teach by posing in front of my classes, demonstrating those frozen picture images that were meant to convey a world of movement and power. I showed off each picture to my students, then moved from one pictured stance to another. After 10,000 hours of working out I was able to do that.

Even with all the strength I developed in all those hours of workouts my movement from one pose to the next hadn't succeeded very well for me *or* for my students. Oh, I'd won some and lost some. My students did too. You've read the results. Still, I wanted more.

Then as we were writing the first draft of this book Carla quite innocently asked me, "Why don't you teach your students to put their hips into their techniques *before* they reach color belt rank?

I frowned at her and thought, "*Say what? Hips?*" That was the way this book *really* started.

Karate dogma provided my first answer to her question. I replied, "Karate is too complicated for students to learn everything at once. They will be overloaded." Even as I mouthed that answer, I knew better. I was looking left and right like a truant child, hoping Carla wouldn't notice my lousy response.

I knew that when you teach someone to do something wrong or partially incorrect it takes *hundreds* of times the initial effort to correct the problems created. That's a perfect answer when secrecy is desired but I wanted to teach the solutions *openly*.

Besides, Carla didn't buy my answer. She was an innocent karate beginner but she wasn't a fool. She knew all about my usual black belt bullying tactics and they were failing miserably with her.

Carla was not only unconvinced; she was skeptical. She told me, "That's B%(($—+! I didn't buy that C%@& answer from my own husband and I certainly won't believe it from *you*, Kyoshi!" She perceived correctly that I didn't know what I was talking about.

In that vein, other students kept asking about hip power. The litany I'd always heard ad nauseam was; "Hit from the hips, use your hips, do it with your hips." Being clueless, I decided to go on a reality hunt.

I watched athletes in other sports and didn't see *any* force that was being generated by their hips. Their power came from their legs and passed *through* their hips into their torsos, then into their arms. Then their power hit the target.

When I compared my observations about other athletes to karate skills, I didn't see any force being *generated* by the hips in karate techniques either. Still, after thirty-five years in the martial arts I wasn't ready to dispute that karate power came from the hips. So I continued to look for answers to the riddle of hip theory.

About that same time Carla asked me to define the word "*set*." The heavens seemed to be conspiring against me, because I didn't have an adequate answer for *that* question either. It's disturbing being found out. Carla was really nailing me (and later I had to thank her.)

Armed with her questions about "hips" and "set" foremost in my mind, I watched my students, other instructors and competitors at tournaments closely for months.

Have you ever had a moment in your life when you were trying to understand something and suddenly the "A-HA" feeling hit you? I did, at that point.

I analyzed what *set* actually does. Of course we hit as hard as possible with it when necessary. But I realized that *three* dynamics are involved with set - *Balance*, *Thrust* and *Impact*. What I discovered about these three dynamics was a revelation.

Chapter Seven

BALANCE

ADAPT

Let's be "upright" here, shall we?

Many years ago when I was learning to ride a bicycle, I discovered the importance of balance. As a beginner I over-steered, hesitated, wobbled and jerked my way along the sidewalks. I needed training wheels on my bike at first, even with my father helping me steer.

Once I mastered balance on the bike I moved from one direction to the next with only subtle corrections. I found that balance serves the same function in karate. When we've mastered balance, we effect a fluid and relaxed transition from one move to the next.

By maintaining balance karate students develop focus. They aim and hit targets while avoiding and blocking attacks. I wondered, "How do we *do* all that?"

We originally learned karate form from the static poses in karate "how to" books, but we couldn't demonstrate movement or incorporate balance by looking at pictures. All we could do was place our feet exactly as the pictures showed, then contort our bodies into reflections of the printed pages.

As a result of our contortions we felt that we were "balanced" whenever we weren't falling down, like the Shodan who imitated the fourth-degree's pictured stance and couldn't move! When training that way we didn't allow for variations in body type, size or strength. We could imitate the poses, but we didn't know how to compensate for individual physiology.

In karate, form was everything. It was the end result rather than a means to an end. My karate program lost a lot of good people because of that

71

mindset. Most of my students couldn't achieve the required athletic form.

Specifically, my own wife dropped out of karate. She told me, "I wanted the protection karate provides and didn't give a damn about form. I certainly never wanted to be like a statue in a picture." She helped me realize that balance and form are inseparable partners, but balance *always* takes precedence over form.

Why is this so? The bicycle example seems to work, so imagine sitting on a bicycle with both feet on the pedals. You're not moving at all. You're stationary - in stance between moves. What keeps you from falling down? Perfect form? Posing hard? I don't think so. Point made - balance is more important than form.

Physically, balance is the application of coordinated strength from all parts of our body. It provides a state of equilibrium between our body's center of mass and gravity.

The lesson we learned from Japanese karate culture about balance was that of "tanden." That's their word for our balance point. For the Japanese and Okinawans, tanden is our center of gravity - and it's where movement begins, according to their theory.

Coincidentally, this point is at hip level. That explains where the notion of hip power comes from in Asian cultures.

Notwithstanding the hip power myth, balance is obvious. Balance is maintained while moving, standing, lying, sitting or leaning. Imagine an old-fashion balance scale. If you put twenty pounds of weight on one side of the scale, you must have twenty pounds of weight on the opposite side to balance the scale.

It's like a kid's "teeter-totter." In karate when we lean as we kick, we are using leg thrust and torso strength to equalize the weight on all sides of the balance point.

Coordinated strength *creates* what we call form, which produces the desired results upon impact. It is the traditional basis for all promotions in karate.

Form is truly defined by the balance, grace and style exhibited when executing techniques.

That was what *really* mattered in karate, and I could teach it to my students. I could also guide my fellow black belt teachers so they could teach those important lessons. How do the different ranks demonstrate balance?

Shodans exhibit balance only when they are in a stance. They have yet to master balance when they move. When I ask them to slow down during training, Shodans typically can't maintain balance when they change stances to apply their techniques.

Shodans use quickness to move from one stance to another without falling. They "shoot" their techniques, as if pedaling fast on a bike. (Moving *slowly* with balance is a more advanced skill.) The strength Shodans gain from their quickness develops into balanced movement.

Nidans repeat techniques, combinations and kata patterns enough to develop muscle strength and memory in all parts of their bodies while moving. They are still learning how to apply balance when actually hitting targets.

Traditionally we learned to "hit the air" during workouts. When we execute techniques into mid-air there is no release of the thrust that moves up from the legs through our body into a target. That energy circulates back into our bodies and builds muscle strength.

How can Nidans develop impact balance by hitting air? They can't. They *have* to hit target pads and bags. Hitting opponents resulted in my personal debacle with injured students when I was a Nidan.

Hit pads instead, it's safer. When we hit pads, half our thrust is released into the target. The other half rebounds from the impact point back into our body as a cycle of energy.

That rebounding energy makes Nidans lose their balance; they bounce off. As they continue hitting, Nidans learn how to adjust and compensate for changes in balance during impact. This compensation develops into Sandan skill.

So, Shodans build muscle memory and strength with repetition of techniques. Nidans learn balanced movement with applied techniques. Up to the Nidan level, students learn how to utilize balance for their own body types and personal abilities.

Sandans have mastered those earlier lessons. They use their own balance effectively and discover how they can take advantage of others' lack of balance. By observing their opponents' positions and movement, Sandans recognize which techniques their opponents can use.

For example, when we lean, half of the techniques we are capable of doing are gone. If you lean to the right you can punch strongly with your left arm and kick with your left leg, but you can't kick with your right leg or punch strongly with your right arm without shifting.

Sandans use this kind of information to force their opponents out of a balanced position. Sandan Billy easily beat Shodan Gary because he recognized that Gary leaned to set up his kicks. When Gary leaned, Billy moved in and forced Gary off-balance. It was child's play for Billy's score because Gary telegraphed his kicks like that.

Since Shodans are off balance while moving and Nidans are off balance while hitting, Sandans can take them to task at any speed. That's what Sandan Peter did to his Shodan students at the tournament. He owned them.

Yondans have even better understanding of opponents' position and movement than Sandans. They have mastered forcing opponents off-balance. This advanced skill is not only effective for counter-attacks, it's the way Yondans set traps.

Yondan Peter set a trap for Shodan Mariana when sparring her at the UNM Karate Club 2000 year-end tournament. He baited her by leaving his arms down. When she punched at his face he slipped the punch, wrapped his arm around her head, then spun and threw her down. He finished his takedown trap with a decisive punch to her midsection. That stunning combination was a volatile revelation to those of us watching.

The ability to analyze information and use it against (or with) opponents is what makes Yondans professional level athletes. Advanced understanding of balance is the key to successful transition for karate application from the dojo to the streets. It allows a stable base from which we can develop thrust and power.

Chapter Eight

THRUST

HOW TO DEVELOP POWER

Let's hit as hard as possible.

I defined thrust as "the energy that starts in a muscle group in one part of the body, then transfers unimpeded to another part of the body until it is discharged on a target, or dissipates into air." (The phrase, "energy discharged on a target" defines *"impact."* It's advanced. We'll get into that later on.)

When I focused on thrust as a single dynamic element, I observed that thrust originated in our leg muscles, *not* our hips. Athletes from all other sports maximized power with their legs.

Boxers Muhammed Ali and Ray Leonard demolished their opponents from the ground up. Football quarterbacks Joe Montana and John Elway stepped forward and launched accurate fifty-yard passes using the thrust of their legs. Baseball batters Mark McGwire and Sammy Sosa knocked home runs four hundred and twenty-feet over ballpark fences using leg force.

Tiger Woods demonstrates the best example of leg thrust; he drives three hundred and fifty-yard golf shots straight down fairways! I found it amazing how Tiger and all those other athletes were using their *legs* to develop and maximize power. That realization contradicted what I had learned in karate.

From an article in a March, 1975 Samurai magazine— which has been out of publication since the late 1970's - I reveal the most pervasive karate myth. The myth of hip power:

> *It is only when the student no longer needs to think about each succeeding movement, that he can begin to apply the next stage of training,*

knowing when and how to focus the muscles of the body at the right time.

Contrary to popular belief, <u>the muscles are not used dynamically in karate</u>, except in special training, <u>to move the limbs of the body into blocking, punching, or kicking motions.</u> They are used to guide the limb toward its intended target and at a certain point, the muscles are contracted, stopping the motion in an instant, allowing the kinetic energy to be transferred into the target. In Japanese this is known as kime (focus). <u>The actual thrusting power</u>, <u>which propels the arm or leg</u>, <u>is generated by the strong torquing action of the hips</u>. This rotation is much the same as swinging a bat or golf club. Smooth and powerful turning of the hips is essential to effective application of power. (Underlining is added.)

The last sentence is true. Many other lines are true as well, but we in karate bought *all* of the ideas presented in that paragraph - and the previous <u>underlined</u> ideas are completely *FALSE*!

If you have taken karate or are in it now, you may disagree. Let me provide a drill that I share with my students to prove my point. First, my students stand with all of their weight on their heels, knees locked and butts tilted back so their lower backs are swayed. I have them lift their shoulders up and stick their heads forward. From this position, they throw punches as hard as they can. Try it.

The exercise is *awful*! That's why I named it the "sucky-punch" drill! Why are the punches so useless? My students could only straighten their arms as they punch. The powerful thrust that their big muscles could contribute was shut down. In this drill my students' major pivot points - the balls of their feet, ankles, knees, hips and shoulders were locked out. No thrust (power) was able to pass through.

When my students hit pads with these punches, all they could do was tap their targets very weakly. Their locked joints couldn't allow thrust generated by muscles in one part of their body to pass unimpeded into other parts of their body. Complete body thrust *couldn't* impact the target.

You may say, "But I've been taught that real power, what you call 'thrust,' comes from the hips like that <u>Samurai</u> magazine article you quoted."

Wrong again, "grasshopper." I was finally becoming a magician like Kwai Chang Cain in the television series "Kung Fu," and I found that thrust passes *through* the hips; it doesn't come *from* the hips. Our hips will impede this progress of thrust unless we open them loosely as a pivot point. That's probably why all of our martial arts ancestors thought power came from their hips. They twitched their hips to augment power from their center mass, but that active "hip twitch" shut off their leg thrust, just as it would with us today.

Think of sprinter Carl Lewis twitching his hips when he explodes out of the starting block. He wouldn't explode out; his hip-twitch spasm would cause him to fall flat on his face!

Or imagine Barry Bonds twitching his hips as he swings his baseball bat. Instead of hitting a home run, he'd be lucky if the ball he tagged would dribble past the infield.

If Tiger Woods tried to use his hips to generate power with his golf swing, he'd have the same results I did. Mistakenly, I tried using my hips to generate power with my golf swing. I drove the golf ball 150 yards forward and 40 yards to the right. I had an *awful* banana slice.

When I realized the importance of leg thrust and applied it to my golf swing, my drives went 240 yards straight down the fairway! That's no Tiger Wood's distance, but it was a major improvement in understanding both golf *and* karate thrust development!

That was what I was seeing in the other athletes. I finally understood that reality was true in karate as well.

I also had to accept that when we use any of our body's pivot points inappropriately, they pinch-off and stop building thrust before it can pass through them. For instance, if you twitch your hips as you punch *no* leg thrust will pass through your hips (anymore than it would with the athletes mentioned.) The resultant punching power comes from only your torso and arm muscles. Both Roger and Roy found that out the hard way.

Roger found that out when he stunned his girlfriend's drunken stepfather with a punch, then had to deal with the subsequent attack. Roy failed to knock out El Seedy in the theater even after two adrenaline bursts and numerous punches. Why?

Roy originally thought that the slanted floor and seats between them prevented him from knocking out El Seedy. Wrong answer. Both Roy and Roger trained by trying to use their hips to generate power. When they twitched their hips they locked out the power thrust from their legs.

All they could hit with was the power in their torsos and arms. That wasn't enough to knock anyone out. Stun yes, knockout, no.

Locking out *any* pivot point diminishes or completely shuts down the thrust you want to pass through it. Our knees, hips and shoulders are less capable of stopping thrust because of their ball and socket nature. Thrust *will* be trapped if our knees are locked, our hips twitched, or our shoulders are raised unnaturally, as in the sucky-punch drill. So how do we let our pivot joints open up?

Relax. All our pivot points must be *allowed* to open loosely in order for thrust to pass through them. How do you know when you've got it right? That's a good question.

Sandan Peter asked me, "When I do a technique I feel like three or four disjointed parts of my body are trying to cooperate and they're not succeeding. Why?" I showed him how to incorporate leg thrust in his moves and he suddenly felt like a missile. His body became one coordinated carbon-based assault weapon!

Peter actually backed off during basic drills after he first learned about leg thrust. He shook his head and moved to the back of the class he was leading.   I asked him, "What's wrong?"

Peter shook his head again and replied, "Wow.   I'm hitting harder than I ever have before and it's freaking me out."   I enjoyed his amazement because I knew he was only moving at *half* speed.   He had a *lot* more to come.

I saw smooth ripples of powerful thrust traveling from his leg muscles through his hips into his torso, then to his arm muscles as he punched.

When all of the pivot points along the energy path open up, thrust continues to build as it passes into the next muscle group along the path.   You can see it develop in any athlete from the ground up when you recognize what you're seeing.   Watch Tiger Woods hit a drive.   He *LASHES* at the ball with totally complete body power!

Using that analogy you may wonder as Peter did, "How exactly does this building thrust influence correct impact on a target?"   That's a good question.

How about another good question.   Does the speed of thrust, coupled with the range of distance that we choose have a major influence on how hard we hit?

Of course it does, and it's obvious in the different black belt ranks!

Chapter Nine

SPEED

DELIVERY

Let's go FULL speed!

The definition of speed may seem obvious, but describing how fast we move and execute techniques is quite daunting. I mused, "Carla, we all feel the energy surge that speed provides, and we see it in others. Speed is a function of applied strength."

Carla frowned and said nothing. I was oblivious to her confusion and continued my diatribe; "I've heard others describe speed by using 23%, 51%, 78%, or 110%, but I don't know what that means. I can't define speed accurately enough to use percentages. Let's use plain old numbers, one through ten instead."

Carla responded, "Oh yeah? Nobody I know *has* ten speeds, not even *YOU*, Kyoshi! *I* only use a couple of settings on my own blender. *One* chops stuff up and *ten* finishes the job."

She had a good point, so we brainstormed together and realized that most people have only *three* speeds: slow, medium and fast. We decided that another bicycle example might be helpful. A three-speed bike could demonstrate the differences in the speeds used by each black belt rank.

We all use slow speeds when learning and teaching new information. When we pedal a bike in first gear it's like walking speed. (If we're completely unfamiliar with what's going on, it's *crawling* speed.)

In first gear we memorize new techniques, patterns, dynamics and applications. We can find the best ways to move.

Second gear on that bicycle gives us the freedom to pedal faster as we steer the handlebars. We use medium speeds after we've become familiar with basic moves by aiming at targets and developing range. It's jogging speed.

During practice we learn how to decelerate from medium speed to slow speed on impact. We put on the brakes or downshift. That results in "feather-touch" contact for safety with partners. What about fast speed?

When we're on a three-speed bike we shift to third gear and pedal hard. We use fast speeds when hitting target pads and bags as we practice for real-life fights and during karate competition. That's running speed.

We can still put on the brakes in third gear, but it's better to stop pedaling and downshift during practice. With partners we maintain safety by moving fast, then decelerating. Again, "feather touch" for safety.

We also use fast speed during actual violent situations in real life. Our techniques must hit chosen targets with appropriate energy for justice to be served during such incidents.

Sandan Roger nailed his girlfriend's stepfather by using fast speed perfectly. During that encounter injuries were minimized and the point was made: *NO* more abuse would be allowed. Roger moved at high speed and felt like God's hand of justice.

There's more. We achieve our fastest speed when adrenaline kicks in and we pedal like crazy toward the finish line. During those times we sprint, fight for our lives, make love and win championships. During those marvelous times we visualize *slowly*, regardless of the actual speed we're moving.

FULL SPEED is the enigma of motion. How can we pedal that bicycle as fast as possible in third gear physically while simultaneously visualizing as slow as possible in first gear mentally?

That's the enigma! The answer isn't easy to understand but it's *obvious* when you've done it. Whenever we are threatened or exhilarated, our adrenal gland shoots a burst of pure chemical energy to our brains.

When adrenaline kicks in we mentally process *all* information at slow speed while at the same time our bodies physically develop *full* speed techniques to deal with the situation.

You may be familiar with scientific theory regarding the fight-or-flee syndrome called the "tachy-psychy effect." Scientists believe that our first cognizance as humans developed in the brain stem. According to this theory, whether we run or fight is an instinctive decision. It's emotional, completely uncontrolled by our conscious thoughts.

Adrenaline causes this full-speed response. It's responsible for the instincts of cave men when they perceived threats. As Steve Irwin, the crocodile hunter from "down under" Australia would say, "Danger! Let's run away! Or stay and fight!"

Maybe we could run *and* fight, but our other senses are blocked out when adrenaline kicks in. Other considerations hold no sway. At full speed, touch, taste and hearing are rendered numb. This numbness enhances visual acuity and allows us to see the world in slow motion as we "do our thing" for survival.

The effects of adrenaline cause us to make decisions so quickly that we don't even remember what we do! Police officers commonly don't remember how many shots they fire in a shoot-out when their first shot doesn't stop an attacker. The cops know their last shot stops the deadly action, but shots in between are a blur.

Racing legend Dale "The Intimidator" Earnhardt exemplified the dangers of full speed. He crashed and died on the last turn of the last lap of the NASCAR 2001 Daytona 500. That's what happens at full speed, because its risks cause crashes.

Yondan Roy's double-dose of adrenaline gave him a heightened sense of slow motion. That allowed him to dodge punches and batter El Seedy full speed in the theater.

In karate practice, full speed causes pulled muscles and sprained joints during solo drills. With partners it results in knockouts and other serious injuries that require hospitalization or surgery. My shoulder and eye operations were a testament to those inherent dangers.

My karate mentors and other successful leaders taught a more positive message. They taught how to control full speed by building confidence. Unless we do that we suffer all the problems fear causes. My personal experience with the thirty "football thugs" during self defense training proved to me that I could ignore fear when going full speed. Even as a beginner I defeated fear and its effects. How did that happen?

I practiced. Practice is *not* training. Most karate training drills are basic stances and "bouncing around" aerobic exercises that hit air. That is physical work.

Real practice involves mental visualization, applying skills with partners and opponents. This is how we develop ability to deal with real enemies.

During practice we help each other as a team. We get it together physically, mentally and spiritually. As black belts, we announce our rank loudly to the entire world by how *appropriately* we respond with speed.

Appropriate speed isn't a function of physical strength. It's a direct result of the way we think. That makes it a deliberate choice. How does speed, both appropriate and inappropriate, manifest in black belt ranks?

Most Shodans aren't comfortable when moving slowly. Using the bicycle example, even as rookie black belts they prefer pedaling at faster speeds.

That sounds contradictory, but it really isn't. Most Shodans use speed to compensate for their lack of confidence, balance and ability to hit hard. Practically all the words on *both* lists provide confusion and frustration for them.

Shodans gain confidence by developing combination techniques. They improve their balance at all speeds by working on the transitions in kata patterns. Their confidence is well earned when they spar with partners. This confidence gains promotion to second-degree rank for them.

Nidans are still learning how to control their "start" and "stop" speed with techniques. High-speed transition pulls Nidans off-balance because they still have those places between moves. Nidan Horace learned that lesson when his tricks didn't work against me. He became discouraged and quit because of his ego. That was a typical Nidan example.

When Nidans miss they have no control. They miss frequently. Ed was a perfect example of "Nidanhood" when he missed and his opponent hit him with a spinning back kick at a tournament. Ed showed poor judgement, yet he compensated and won.

The Thinker had complete control over fear from personal threat, as evidenced by the park scenario against the seven toughs. Had any of those "park scum" moved, he knew he could beat them. *All* Nidans develop this certainty that their speed will beat attackers even when such certainty is unfounded.

When second-degrees feel this certainty for the first time in practice they have no confusion about their skills, which are excellent. They ignore fear. Ultimately their certainty isn't enough but it works well until they ask two questions.

Their first question is "Hey! Why is my partner knocked out? I didn't hit him hard. I was moving slowly." Their second question is "Why isn't my speed fast enough?" Both are classic examples of the tachy-psychy effect!

Nidans approach these questions very carefully, because they aren't used to feeling uncertain. The answers lead to Sandan rank.

Sandans recognize when they are off-balance and compensate by changing speed with purpose, even when they miss. They shift their weight and body angle by using their knees as pistons to regain equilibrium.

That's how Sandan Peter was able to beat his Shodan students so easily at the tournament. Shodans and Nidans can't handle this Sandan ability to change speed and acquire new targets.

Fourth-degrees *master* those skills, but in so doing they often have to come to grips with another problem. Yondan Peter complained about his sparring partners during practice. When he sparred at medium speed, they lashed out and occasionally hit him too hard. His partners were frustrated because they knew that he had the ability to throw endless combinations.

Peter could identify each target even before it opened up. (I promise to reveal how he manages that feat later in the chapter on focus.) But imagine the frustration Peter's partners had. He could and *did* score on them at will. The only way they could keep up with him was to hit him! They had to hit any perceived target as fast as possible.

Their full speed reaction is incredibly dangerous and hard to control safely. Shodans and Nidans touch only the surface level of this speed because of their inexperience.

I told Peter, "When you spar junior black belts you overwhelm them. They're threatened." Peter blinked, visualizing what I said as I continued, "That's when most people quit, because the only way they can hold you off is to belt you one. *These* students aren't quitting."

Both Peter *and* his students were reacting to dangerous speed in basic human ways. In karate we all practice together and develop those reactions into trained responses.

With practice we foster our mental acuity and muscle memory so we can deal quickly with danger. Our modified responses let us have the best possible conclusion to *any* violent encounter - namely, one in which *WE* win and the bad guys lose, as fast as possible.

That's why we practice with partners. Peter was developing his advanced Yondan requirements for varying speeds as necessary. His students didn't have the skill to keep up with him and he knew it. They knew that he knew it.

I told him, "Your students aren't stupid. They know they can't keep up with you. They score deliberately and go too fast even though it's dangerous and inappropriate. That's why they occasionally hit you too hard."

"Right. Go figure," Peter replied as he winked at me. He understood completely. Peter successfully taught full speed while learning it for his fourth-degree requirements. Yondans teach all of that to their students in order to master it for themselves.

Shodan Mariana didn't like the way Peter taught. She wasn't advanced enough to understand fourth-degree black belt assignments, and she resisted Peter's tips for her improvement. He was developing his requirements for varied speeds when practicing. He was teaching Mariana those advanced speed skills while he was learning them.

Peter simplified his lofty tasks into discreet steps to better his own understanding. By doing so he helped Mariana learn his skills despite her resistance.

With those skills she broke the typical Shodan mold by winning the 2000 United States Karate Alliance Woman's Grand Championship in Sparring. She beat a couple of her higher ranking opponents 5 points to 0, and successfully defended her title in 2001!

That was formidable development in skill that Peter challenged Mariana to attain. She rose to the occasion. She transcended fast speed and *sprinted* full-speed with her techniques to achieve safety in practice with her friends. She pedaled *all-out* on that three-speed bike!

I was thrilled! Peter achieved even more than we imagined possible. Mariana developed advanced black belt skills, attitudes and spirit *long* before she would be promoted to higher ranks.

Mariana was only a Shodan, but she was *doing* Yondan level skills! The impact of her achievement was a wonder to behold. The Black Belt molds were being broken. The secrets were being exposed, and it was about time.

During karate practice we maintain correct speed for safety with each other to prevent injuries. (Let's hit hard, but we won't hit *each other* too hard. Only the bad guys are going to get hurt.) You remember the phrase "energy discharged on a target?" Thrust causes speed, and speed develops impact.

Chapter Ten

IMPACT

PAYLOAD

Hit something that deserves it!

As the truths about *thrust* and *speed* were revealed to me, I shared them with my evening karate club at the University of New Mexico. The results were astounding.

After the frustration of the "sucky-punch" drill, I shared a second exercise that is *much* more empowering. Try *this* exercise to trace the thrust route for the most powerful punches obtainable, as my students did.

My students stand lightly, with their weight balanced just behind the balls of their feet. Right-handed students put their left foot forward. Lefties have their right foot in front. I have them punch with their strong arm. Traditionally these are called "reverse" punches.

I prefer to name these strikes "natural punches" because as we walk we naturally swing our right arm forward as we step forward with our left foot and vice versa. This relates to our bodies' tendency to automatically seek balance. Our best punches will be a result of that natural balance and dynamic leg strength.

I asked my students to execute natural punches using only their arm muscles. I had them add the muscles of their shoulders. When they added the rotation of their torso and hips, the sound of their punches went from a "tap" to a "pop" as they hit the pads.

Then I asked them to *push* with their rear leg muscles and prayed, "*Please* let their thrust pass cleanly through their hips. *No* twitching."

The sound of my students hitting those pads increased to a loud "*BAM*" due to the acceleration of thrust.   As they continued practicing their accuracy and penetration improved and their confidence soared.

I had each student concentrate on pushing with their rear leg, causing their front knee to flex.   The toes of both feet grip the floor.   Both ankles flex as the calf muscles come into play.   Weight is shifted forward as the front knee bends.   This causes the front thigh to tighten and doubles the thrust of power being supplied by the rear leg.

All miraculous power supplied by both legs from the ground up is multiplied by the flexing of both buttocks as the waist turns loosely and naturally when the rear hip is shoved forward by the straightening rear leg.   The building thrust passes cleanly through the hips into the torso.

The stomach muscles tighten as the torso turns, and the back and chest muscles flex.   This torso flex builds thrust into the rear shoulder.   As the rear shoulder is driven forward, its muscles add thrust to the punching arm.   The arm muscles add thrust as it straightens.   The elbow pivot-point opens and the still increasing thrust passes through that joint into the forearm. ·

The muscles of the forearm flex and turn the wrist in a corkscrewing motion.   The hand clenches at the moment the fist makes contact with the target.

To amplify the upper body torque, the lead (front) hand is pulled back to the waist as the rear hand punch is thrown.   This amplification provides the development of the most practiced technique in *every* karate school in the world, the rear elbow strike!

Okay, so we in karate are paranoid.   We practice *most* against an attack coming from behind us!   That has been useful.

Our entire body provides power, which then discharges full force into the target.   It's that "kinetic energy transfer" deal.   When the muscles of the body are tightened upon impact, just imagine a cement block landing on a target.

I had the privilege of observing such impact in practice.   In the course of this *one* class I saw a one hundred percent improvement in *every* rank, from beginner through black belt. Such results in a single class were unprecedented and quite astounding to witness.

At the end of the evening, the students' naturally developed punches were hitting with resounding "thuds." I felt like I was watching a <u>Batman</u> movie. All I needed to hear were some "biffs, pows, and bops!"

The students learned to hit very heavy-handed while using only about half of their top speed. More force would have injured the shoulders of the teachers holding the pads. When more speed *is* used, however, it will turn the sound of impact into a solid, "Whomp!" (Do *that*, Batman!)

Even with that successful class, I needed more input. When I demonstrated leg thrust to another Sandan he made an interesting observation. He told me, "Kyoshi, in the middle black belt ranks we are aware that when we connect with a target, the impact compression rebounds back through our bodies all the way down to our feet." He was right.

When the rebounding compression from impact traces back along it's original route, it completes a cycle of energy. The thrust at impact starts in the feet, builds in the legs, torso, arms, (etc.,) then rebounds from the striking point back through the body and ends once again in the feet. Our feet, planted firmly with our toes gripping the floor, stabilize the thrust as it hits and penetrates the target.

Upon impact, thrust completes the cycle of compression, and the power created develops a reaction in our body's muscles similar to a gyroscopic effect. The thrust lashes out, as with Tiger Woods golf-swing, because our leg muscles enhance karate power by pushing against the earth's gravity.

I think Tiger Wood's golf swing is a result of his child-like attempts to equal his father's drives. As a boy Tiger would try to match his dad's distance off the tee, and somehow was never discouraged when he failed. His father always encouraged him; it was always a good try. Tiger just "swung away."

90

Now he's won numerous major golf championships by using his natural child's golf swing as an adult. As black belts, that's what we try to do. We just swing away and we hopefully mature as well as Tiger has!

What about the difference in black belt ranks regarding speed and thrust? As stated before, Shodans have to develop the right kind of leg strength to maintain balance while moving.

Since thrust is initiated in the legs, Shodans' relatively weak leg muscles inhibit their ability to hit with maximum force even with single techniques. First- degrees need to practice combinations and hit target pads with their moves.

By doing that they learn to adjust their balance to compensate for the compression caused by the circle of thrust. Their legs get stronger with the stances they develop during such training. They may look like statues, but they can move!

Nidans are capable of hitting with maximum thrust when executing techniques because they've hit physical targets repeatedly. Achieving balanced thrust while doing combinations is more difficult. They are still learning how to coordinate the rebounding effects of thrust as they make the transition from the stopping point at impact to the next move.

The cure for this Nidan ailment is the same prescription dispensed for Shodans, with a twist. Nidans have to continue hitting pads with combinations. That will teach them how to adjust their balance and compensate for thrust rebound.

Here's a riddle for you. What do you call a Nidan who has practiced combinations repeatedly until they're controlled and balanced? A Sandan!

Remember the "connected carbon-based assault weapon?" He's a Sandan. His thrust is becoming so completely coordinated that his entire body feels like a missile locked on to the target. To promote to higher ranks, all black belts must pass through the initial feelings of confusion, uncertainty and doubt until they accept their own excellence.

Yondans are *masters* of balanced movement. They are *comfortable* with it. Their joints, the pivot points that transmit balanced powerful thrust, open like hinges as their bodies' power drives through them to the points of impact on chosen targets.

Just after impact, the contracting muscles finish flexing and because of the resultant energy rebound, the gyroscopic effect of thrust continues to build. Why? Because the muscles that stop the movement at impact create more thrust which rebounds back along the energy channels in the body, as mentioned earlier by the Sandan.

This *isn't* mystic at all. It's physical dynamics. One form of thrust *penetrates* the target at impact and a second less obvious form of thrust moves back through the body *during* impact.

That more subtle form of thrust rebounds and generates the secondary energy for our *next* moves that will strike, block or kick our chosen targets. Even with fourth-degree skill, precise execution is *meaningless* if appropriate energy isn't discharged into the desired target at impact.

For Yondans' next promotion, they must discharge energy appropriately. This requires advanced, intimate understanding of applied contact. The only way to have that is through focused vision.

Chapter Eleven

<u>FOCUS</u>

SEE IT!

What are YOU looking at?

Karate isn't life or death, is it? I realized karate is *more* than life or death. It is unconditional acceptance.

In terms shown by recent Hollywood movies, the best of empty-hand karate here in the United States combines uniquely American <u>Tombstone</u> wild-west flair with the intense African <u>Ghost and the</u> <u>Darkness</u> animal gaze, European <u>Saving Private Ryan</u> war reality, and futuristic <u>Matrix</u> "bullet-time" speed with vision. <u>Gladiator,</u> which won the Oscar for best picture in 2001 is the "sword-and-sandal take" on Hollywood's focus. Take a look at those movies.

I took a gander at these movies with respect to karate. (OK, so I watched these videos *very* closely.) Then I simplified, clarified, organized and amplified the concepts I saw and applied them to karate. I already *knew* this stuff, but I needed a good visual basis for my expansion of accepted fact.

That process helped identify successful people who show the best results. They attain significance by focusing on what really works. I wanted the best destiny for my students, so I taught them how to achieve their best efforts. To do that they had to focus.

I discovered something *very* important about the power of sight when I learned how to ride a bicycle many years ago in 1953. When I stared at a rock that I wanted to miss, I *always* ran over it. (It was a *terrible* bump…ouch!)

I missed those rocks in the road by focusing on a path that went *around* them. Potholes were even worse than the rocks because they drew me in. Those voids were magnetic when I pedaled my bike.

I applied mature karate tests to what was learned in my youth about riding bicycles and realized that our minds must conceive targets first, but our eyes *always* lead the way. Our vision has to stay locked on the chosen target until techniques are fully completed.

That was the way Mel Gibson portrayed vision in the movie The Patriot when he told his sons, "Aim small, miss small." It was a powerful moment.

Ready, aim and fire. That is the essence of focus. No distractions are allowed. Rocks and potholes can't be acknowledged. After preparation we focus on a target, then punch, kick or block. We shoot our gun, loose our arrow, hit or throw the ball and complete each move.

Then we acknowledge or celebrate results, correct or readjust aim, recuperate, or make ready. Thus we deal with "ferocious wild animals" as Gichin Funakoshi mentioned in his book.

We apply each technique and then look at the next target zone one at-a-time. Every winner knows this. Every loser is either dead, or they know that they don't know it. All of us who have lost and aren't dead must learn to focus.

The secret is full-speed visual acuity. When adrenaline kicks in we must keep a keen eye and aim precisely for each target, nail it, then aim at and hit the next target.

Adrenaline blocks out our senses of touch, taste and hearing. Those faculties are desensitized. Adrenaline causes very advanced applications and the results are incredible. Steven Spielberg's movie Saving Private Ryan showed adrenaline reality to perfection during the intense battle sequences, which were perceived in slow motion.

Life is a slow process, much like forging a samurai sword or creating a diamond. Imagine how *long* it takes a piece of charcoal to be heated and squashed into a diamond. Even with a master's degree in geology I didn't understand the importance of this until I defined focus as absolutely clear and totally committed vision. With focus our attention concentrates on one distinct and sharply defined target.

You remember the example of the Ghost and the Darkness lions in the Tsavo River valley in Africa? Those man-eaters were never distracted from their goal. They simply went for their targets. Their targets were human prey. Those lions created total carnage, a worst-case scenario of death. I didn't want that. I wanted my best life by *preventing* that.

There are more positive examples provided by successful people in all walks of life. Mother Theresa is a magnificent example of spiritual guidance. She helped people cope with death.

Bill Gates exemplifies the best way to develop business and computers by helping people with high technology. I identify with him because my father was an inspired genius who helped invent computer wizardry.

I also acknowledge God's excellence in my own life from my Mom's example. My mother's remarkable kind of courage shows up rarely. She showed me how to deal with pain by enduring a twenty-year bout with rheumatic fever. Her lengthy tolerance for pain taught me supreme patience. She taught me to have compassionate tolerance for victims, but *no* patience for losers who complain; they earned what they have. We can see this phenomenon on television ad nauseam. No thanks; as for myself I want significance.

Quickly: name three Nobel peace-prize laureates or three people who influenced your life the most. Which list could you name more quickly? We all know who influenced us significantly. These people contributed their passion and focus to us. These courageous heroes exhibited the results of that aforementioned Ghost and the Darkness gaze.

Admittedly, that particular example is destructive. That is precisely the point. Focus is a self-fulfilling prophecy. Our attention will be focused on either positive or negative results. To achieve the best results we must focus on the best results.

Howard Hill did that with bows-and-arrows and became the most accomplished archer who ever lived. Barry Bonds surpassed Mark MacGwire to become baseball's homerun king. Michael Jordan did it in basketball, Pele' in soccer, Wayne Gretsky in hockey, Muhammed Ali in boxing, Jack Nicklaus and Tiger Woods in golf.

They all developed their "mind's eye best" with their vision. Their desires were so great that they had no thoughts when simply training. Yes, really. For them, practiced efforts surpassed training and internalized successful responses. For them, vision became reality.

Zen mystics call it "mind of no mind." I prefer to call it "mind of pure vision." Champions who use it are heated in competition and crushed under the pressure of their own vision. The majestic success these best winners achieve is heightened by the tachy-psychy effect.

Their constantly practiced mind of pure vision is augmented by adrenaline, which causes their guided action to explode. They don't need to think when they explode because they have constantly practiced mentally, physically and spiritually to ignore distractions. Only the winning results are clear to them. They do what it takes to achieve those results. Their reasons why are crystal-clear.

Watch them as I did. How else can we explain such success? Evaluation of karate black belt focus is a relatively simple matter when compared to that rare excellence.

How does focus manifest in Shodans' eyes? Their attitude is revealed by the introspection detected in their gaze as they think, "I'm not getting this yet but I'm gonna keep on trying."

That's admirable. Ralph had this gaze when he thought about the challenges he had with his Sensei.

This gaze is accompanied by a slight physical hesitation caused when Shodans analyze the feeling of dynamics and application of their moves. They successfully execute techniques but are still unsure of correct application and range.

Shodans want appropriate application like Sandan Roger had at the movie with El Seedy. How can Shodans know appropriate use of moves?

They can't. They haven't been in karate long enough. Shodans need more time to learn how to use techniques appropriately. Sorry about that, but that's life.

When Shodans acknowledge this they don't like it; as a result their "trailing eyes" reveal their insecurity. Their eyes move off-target before they complete techniques. This "look-away" is caused by thinking about what they are doing and trying to figure out what to do next. Looking away from the primary target causes them to move too fast. Commonly, they focus on their next target before they've nailed the first one.

Many times Shodans don't look at the proper target at all because they're too busy trying to remember the correct pattern, dynamics, or the way to use moves. This can lead to further problems if Shodans fail to get constructive instruction. They stagnate when teachers don't know how to guide them.

First-degrees need encouragement and positive help, *not* destructive or punitive criticism. My own karate mentor, Jim Hawkes, always gave me perfect support, acceptance and guidance.

Many students I drove away with my unrealistic standards went to my mentor and flourished as black belts because I didn't offer perfect support—but I digress.

Ralph and Alice dropped out of karate for a different reason. Their egos wouldn't let them accept the help of a mentor because they thought they knew it all.

The Shodans who were beaten by Sandan Peter at a tournament were humble and aware enough to be encouraged by his superior excellence. They knew they didn't know it all and stayed in karate anyway. They continued their development and accepted their mentor's advice. By doing that they became Nidans.

What do Nidans' eyes show? They reveal a confident, devilish delight. A typical second-degree's attitude is, "Hey, I've trained hard and this really works! All of this is paying off."

Unfortunately, Nidans haven't figured out the difference between training and practice. They are capable with good training dynamics but have limited practice in application skills.

That's why they miss and get hit so often. Their eyes reveal great confidence with the tricks that they've mastered. Horace demonstrated that when he challenged me.

Then his challenge failed. Give Nidans anything that is unfamiliar or outside their comfort zones and their eyes develop shutters. What's going on behind the shutters?

Nidans are trying to figure out how they can apply what they already understand to new information. Horace experienced complete confusion when he couldn't score any of his best tricks on me.

It's too bad he quit. Accepting that confusion would have led to his next promotion. The shutters finally come off with Sandans. Their thoughts are "OK, I'm confused. That's part of what I'm doing. Let's get *ON* with this!" Their eyes pierce their targets without a second thought, but a small degree of hesitation may still be present because they continually analyze information.

This constant analyzing eventually develops mental acuity. Sandans realize the focus range is quite narrow with Shodans and Nidans. Sandans are developing a broader cone of vision that gives them the ability to observe peripherally while striking directionally.

That's why Peter's Shodan partners were completely stymied when they sparred him in class and at tournaments. With his broad cone of vision he was learning to identify potential targets before they were open to attack. He exploited those opportunities. This exceptional skill makes it difficult to track where Sandans will strike.

The Sandan moviegoer had that advantage during his encounter with the five "Trans Am toughs" outside the theater. He walked away from potential violence. Had it been necessary his response would have been unpredictable, focused and deadly.

Sandans have enough experience to adapt to a continuous flow of new hostile or violent information and deal with it quickly. The moviegoer demonstrated that as well. His awareness of surroundings and options allowed him to confidently maintain competent safety when walking away from the Trans Am toughs. He knew what he could do to them if they tried anything.

Yondans maintain the piercing concentration of Sandan rank but their cone of vision increases substantially. As a result their hesitation disappears.

Why? Yondans think, "I'm used to this confusion. It's not bad. I not only see all of my opponents' targets, I can simultaneously detect all of their abilities as well!"

Yondans overcome opponents' skills while compensating for their own shortcomings, injuries and weaknesses. Yondan Peter felt that exhilaration when he surprised his fourth- degree buddy with an unexpected move. He felt it again when he baited Mariana with the takedown trap.

Fourth-degrees have to take that vision to another level if they want to progress. I had the privilege of teaching one karate student who became a Yondan. He also learned to lead police SWAT and Dog Teams. After that he led Bomb Squads. His progression was uncanny. He had a sixth sense about karate and life.

Do you believe in a sixth sense? Fifth-degrees do and they use it. In addition to what their wide-open cone of vision perceives Godans "see what cannot be seen." Their sixth sense allows them to fully appreciate and utilize the other five senses. That's what Yondans must develop to become fifth-degree "super professionals."

Now, how is that possible? They practice a more complete awareness of all their senses; sight… smell…touch… hearing…taste…

Yondan Peter used his sixth-sense intuition to acknowledge a brown belt student who tried to sneak up on him at the exact time I was writing this section of the book. He used it another time to prevent an out-of control student from hurting him.

Peter was acting as a helping sensei, and sparred his student with medium speed and light contact. The student threw a full-speed, full-power spinning jump sidekick on purpose at Peter's chest. The student was so out of control that his kick hit Peter in the chin! Peter was stunned but unhurt.

No harm, no foul? Not exactly - it was both harm *and* foul! Peter was wearing a facemask. That and his fourth- degree skills protected him. Peter then proceeded to try and educate the errant student by increasing his own effort to *medium* speed and power.

The student was overwhelmed and couldn't compete. Later he said, "I knew I made a mistake when Sensei Peter stepped on my head."

Peter could have severely injured that helpless student. He didn't. As a budding fifth-degree Sensei he protected his student, even when the student didn't understand the lesson in safety and manners. (Isn't teamwork and trust amazing?)

Yondans want to learn how to listen to the still, small quiet voice we all have which guides us to the right action with conscience. That's how they can ignore ego, fear, hate, pain and ignorance. Consider that this sixth sense is a unique blend of our senses working in harmony to block out distractions.

Yondans want that sixth sense for total control. Fifth-degrees don't care about that. They use their intuitively combined perceptions to analyze their surroundings even when they don't perceive disturbances directly. With time and maturity their heightened perception results in a relaxed state of harmony.

Chapter Twelve

<u>HARMONY</u>

TOTALITY

All the elements come together here.

"Well," you're thinking, "harmony aside, all that information about ranks, dynamics, execution and focus is very interesting, but I'm still confused." I knew you would be and I apologize. I'm sorry.

No, actually I'm *not* sorry! When I first started writing this book I was a sixth-degree black belt. My mission at that rank was to create chaos and abuse confusion. I did that because after thirty years I was bored with the sameness of workouts and competition. That's the rank. The abuse was entertaining and provided distraction for me.

I've noted the same in others but I had no right to inflict my devious boredom on them, even though it seemed to go with the territory. For example, one of my Shodans proudly announced that he was developing circular techniques to have "flow" in his moves. I regarded his statement and told him, "That won't give you flow." He wondered what I meant so I showed him the non-stop continual movement that actually constitutes true flow; it's like a river. I showed that in slow motion.

The shodan recognized the difference between his circular attempts and true flow and exclaimed, "That's just great. I see what you're doing, but *I can't do it!*" He was completely frustrated. Too bad - I knew he would eventually develop flow with practice.

I also realized that I had transcended my "abuse of confusion" stage. I was awarded my seventh-degree black belt at that point. I was frustrating my students at the same time that I ended their confusion. What a deal!

I tired of all that and decided to end both the confusion *and* the frustration. How could I do that? By creating a coherent language describing the way karate actually works.

That had been tried before, of course. In the late 1980's when karate tournaments were rampant I judged competitions on a regular basis. On one such occasion the tournament director gave my panel of judges the following instructions: pointing at each of us in turn he said, "You judge speed, you judge form, you judge the totality of the form, you judge power, and you judge focus."

He had a great idea except for one *huge* detail. None of the other four judges had a clue! Of course we all nodded agreement and proceeded to judge the way we had always judged competitive forms. We voted the highest scores to competitors who did what we liked the most, as usual.

I knew it because as chief judge I had to monitor the others. The one who was supposed to evaluate "power" gave high scores to competitors who showed *no* power, but did have speed and form. The other judges were obviously *not* looking at their assignments either.

In retrospect my friend was onto something important, but he'd given us an assignment without adequate information or instruction. What did he mean by speed? How did form really contribute? What were the aspects that should be considered for totality? What were the considerations for power, or focus?

A decade later I was still at odds with those words. I did find correct answers after searching for the right terms to describe the best visualizations - I learned.

I could demonstrate and teach what I learned but I needed to define a useful language. That was critical. I had to explain what I knew in precise, visually accessible detail. (Maybe soft-selling the more gruesome parts.) Hopefully my definitions have been detailed appropriately in previous chapters of this book.

I began my definitions at a business convention in Utah where Peter Vidmar gave a motivational speech. He's a gymnastic champion from the 1984 Olympics in Los Angeles, who detailed the necessary requirements to go from a "technically perfect" performance which could score only 9.40, to what is needed for a perfect 10.00!

Peter Vidmar's speech and demonstration tasks judges in *all* athletics. From my notes about his speech I accepted that any world class performance done with perfect form will score only 9.40. He showed that to score higher we have to add the elements of *risk*, *originality* and *virtuosity*.

With those elements added, our martial arts grow dramatically. In karate we have life and death, "yin-yang," opposites attracting. At the very heart of karate we see varying degrees of harmony demonstrating risk, original thinking and virtuous excellence. We easily discern when someone is performing in harmony but are unable to explain what we are looking at. "It's cool."

To understand what is seen, we need to define the various elements creating harmony. The chapters on dynamics, balance, thrust, speed, impact and focus hopefully provide the necessary definitions.

Harmonious use of vision is balanced, focused and powerful. Again, it's cool. It is the heart of karate. When we practice outside that "heart" we often observe discord that disrupts harmony.

I have a Rokudan (sixth-degree black belt) karate brother who one evening happened to be standing in line behind three individuals at a checkout counter. The two men and one woman were loud and vulgar as they harassed the cashier. She requested age identification for the liquor they were trying to buy.

My friend distracted the punks by saying, "Hey! Guys! Act more like adults and the cashier might not have to ask you for your ID, you know?"

The distraction worked. The punks glared at my friend and left the store without further ado. The relieved cashier told him, "Thank you! I was really getting scared."

He consoled her by saying, "It was nothing. Really." Of course the punks were waiting for my friend outside the store. He had his arms full of grocery bags, which he laid aside.

Sure enough, one of the little fellas was feeling lucky. He apparently had some knowledge of karate; enough at least to squat low in a deep stance and make some interesting gestures with his hands. He was also feeling quite plucky as he snarled, "I'm gonna tear you a new one, old man."

After winning hundreds of karate tournaments this situation definitely looked quite familiar. My friend was well prepared with balance, focus, and harmony. Ah yes, the elixirs of life in another defining moment. He remembers thinking, "Where have I see this before?"

The punk's spinning back kick might have connected if my friend hadn't first nailed his groin with a mean counter sidekick. The impact of the groin kick caused the punk's knees to collapse, then smash onto the asphalt. It was devastating to the lost soul.

My Rokudan friend walked past the wiped-out agonized punk slowly and asked, "Does anyone *else* want some of this?" He put the groceries in his car.

He heard the loser's girlfriend hiss, "That gray-haired old man just kicked your ass!" She added insult to injury. Her observation was more devastating than my friend's kick!

That encounter *demonstrates* pure balance, focus and harmony. Justice with vision was a direct result!

When we have vision for our best lives, our faith doesn't need black belt degrees. I found *that* out as a seventeen-year-old in high school when my rage diffused a dangerous situation with a football thug.

It took me a long time to realize and understand that God's creative power in our lives is real. I only needed the faith of a trusting child to let it happen.

Notes

GARY PURDUE

Index

About the Author

Gary Purdue received his black belt in 1969. He has been a police officer and reserve deputy sheriff, and was a hand-to-hand, baton and firearms instructor for the Bernalillo County, New Mexico Sheriff Reserves during the mid-1980s.

More than six thousand people, including police and military personnel, have attended his karate program at the University of New Mexico. His students have earned countless trophies and awards, including state, national and world championships. Over three hundred of his students have achieved the rank of first-degree black belt or higher.

He has two previous works published. His own awards number over two hundred, including United States Karate Alliance World Master's Form Champion (1990), and membership in the prestigious Trias International Society and Alliance Hall of Fame. He is counted among the Living Legends of karate.

He lives with his wife, Donna, and enjoys the close relationship with his daughter, son-in-law, brother and mother in Albuquerque, N.M.